WARRIORS OF THE ANCIENT GREEK WORLD

For Valerie and Reenie, your patience is saint like, your support endless. Merci

WARRIORS OF THE ANCIENT GREEK WORLD

A VISUAL GUIDE TO THE PANOPLIES OF WAR

KEVIN L GILES

Pen & Sword

MILITARY

First published in Great Britain in 2022
by Pen & Sword Military
An imprint of
Pen & Sword Books Ltd
Yorkshire - Philadelphia

ISBN 978 1 52677 876 5

Printed and bound by Printworks Global Ltd, London/Hong Kong.

Pen & Sword Books Limited incorporates the imprints of Atlas, Archaeology, Aviation, Discovery, Family History, Fiction, History, Maritime, Military, Military Classics, Politics, Select, Transport, True Crime, Air World, Frontline Publishing, Leo Cooper, Remember When, Seaforth Publishing, The Praetorian Press, Wharncliffe Local History, Wharncliffe Transport, Wharncliffe True Crime White Owl and After the Battle.

For a complete list of Pen & Sword titles please contact

PEN & SWORD BOOKS LIMITED
47 Church Street, Barnsley, South Yorkshire, S70 2AS, England
E-mail: enquiries@pen-and-sword.co.uk
Website: www.pen-and-sword.co.uk

or

PEN AND SWORD BOOKS
1950 Lawrence Rd, Havertown, PA 19083, USA
E-mail: Uspen-and-sword@casematepublishers.com
Website: www.penandswordbooks.com

CONTENTS

FOREWORD

The ancient Greek world and its mighty heroes have proven irresistible material for writers and film makers for centuries. From Homer's *Illiad* to the Hollywood blockbuster movies of today. These warrior heroes have been portrayed in a multitude of ways, clad in fanciful (if not ridiculous) costumes and armour, carrying fantastical weapons and fighting with superhuman strength against innumerable devilish enemies. But what did the fighting men and women of the fifth and fourth centuries BC really look like when waging war? Well, without the aid of a time machine no one will ever truly know but I do think it's safe to rule out leather underpants!

Greek vase paintings, frescos, sculptures, and mosaics offer sound visual evidence as to what they wore and carried in combat. But even these stunning ancient works of art carry a degree of artistic license and propaganda or are simply lacking in the all-important details. Yet the sands of time have not eroded or hidden all the evidence. Stunning artefacts have survived. These remaining examples of armour, weapons and clothing shine the light of truth onto the panoply of war carried and worn by the different peoples of ancient Mediterranean, Middle East and vast Eurasian steppe.

I set out to depict the book's eight different warriors in as much detail and character as possible. Not machine polished or workshop fresh, they are blooded, worn out, sun-faded and caked in the dust and grime of battle. They are intended to be snapshots from antiquity, a kind of attempt at time travelling, minus the DeLorean.

When I was a boy of six or seven years my grandmother gave me a little old book about history's great battles. It had the simplest artwork showing the Greek armies at Troy, the Battle of Agincourt, the victory at Waterloo and a WW2 dogfight between Japanese and US aircraft at the Battle of Midway. I loved to look at the illustrations; as basic as the old hardback was, it filled my head with questions and fuelled my imagination. I learned a lot from that little book.

I believe a good history book should inspire, captivate, educate, and encourage the reader. I hope that this little book of my own ticks these four boxes.

K L GILES.

Kevin Giles has been working in the British film industry as a costume prop specialist for over twenty-three years. He studied Costume Design at London's world-famous Wimbledon School of Art earning a BA Hons degree, graduating in 2000.

He has been involved in producing costume props for well over forty major Film and TV productions, credited and uncredited. Specializing in Costume Armour and Leatherwork, he has worked under some of film's finest award-winning costume designers. Kevin's credits include *No Time to Die* (2021), *Ready Player One* (2018), *Wonder Woman* (2017), Marvel's *Avengers, Age of Ultron* (2015) and *Guardians of the Galaxy* (2014) to name a few. A full list of his film work can be seen on IMDB.com, you can also follow Kevin's work on Instagram @kevin_giles77. Kevin's interests include ancient history, natural history and travel.

ACKNOWLEDGEMENTS

While I knew this project would be a mountain of work to climb, I can tell you it has felt more like climbing the entire Himalayas at times. But, as any mountain climber will tell you, it's worth it!

My journey up this mountain chain was not a lonely one. While I can turn my hand to most things, I am not a Jack of all trades. This is where I called on the help and wisdom of some of the world's finest creative experts, artists and crafts people that I have the pleasure of knowing and working with. Their talents and knowledge are far superior to my own, and without their generosity, time and patience, the fruits of my labour would be far less juicy.

The photography (without which you would not be reading my words), is the work of one of those very artisans who has been on board this project from the start, Oliver May. His remarkable photos and outstanding talent have been fundamental in giving this book its professional weight and class.

The book's design and art editing are the exceptional work of Katy Miller, who has worked tirelessly to give this book its unique look, something fresh, exciting and inspiring. Without her excellent creative and artistic flair, you would again not be reading these words. I would also like to thank costume graphic artist Caroline Lindop for her help enhancing the colour illustrations and for her technical and creative skills, which enabled other elements to be created for the book.

Thank you to Andrew Dow and Grant Perman at FBFX for their support and aid over the years.

A huge thank you to Sarah Moore, amazing expert dyer and textile artist for helping a colour-blind northener get the warriors looking authentic.

And for the fantastic SFX make-up on the Spartan I must thank the extraordinary talent of Max Payn, whose work hammered home the drama of the famous 300's last stand.

To all those other friends and colleagues who aided me in the ascent of this mountain of a project I offer my deepest and heartfelt thanks. Your willingness to help has been truly humbling. I can only hope my passion and determination matches your efforts and does justice to them. You are all brilliant.

Thanks are also due to the models: Glen, Louise, Richard, Evan, Aman, Crispin, Lee and Nivek.

INTRODUCTION

Warfare in the ancient Greek world of the fifth and fourth centuries BC was an extremely high-stakes and violent affair. On the endless Eurasian steppe and deserts of the East, the mounted archer and bowman were supreme in war.

The nomadic horse cultures of the Scythian world developed highly effective mounted guerilla warfare, favoring razor-sharp attacks by swift, skilled riders to large, drawn-out battles on foot. The extreme mobility of the horse and the power of their bows enabled their fearsome military influence to span great distances at lightning speeds.

The mountains and highlands of the Thracian tribal regions created robust light infantry and flexible mounted troops, ideal for rapid deployments and rough terrain.

The Greeks city-states developed disciplined, heavy-infantry-dominated spear warfare to dominate their local rivals in battle. This superior heavily armoured infantry was often recruited to fight far from home by foreign powers.

A later development in Greek infantry warfare saw the introduction of a longer, heavier spear by King Philip II of Macedonia, which in turn pushed the evolution of the infantryman and how he was employed on the battlefield. On Philip's death in 336 BC, his son, the young military genius Alexander the Great, took this new style of infantry east with his elite cavalry, where they were instrumental in defeating Darius's Persian Empire.

The Persian kings themselves would field massive armies filled with eclectic troop types from all corners of their empire: heavily armoured cavalry, endless ranks of archers and spearmen, Greek mercenary infantry, Arabian camel cavalry, Scythian riders, scythed chariots – even conjuring monstrous Indian war elephants from the far reaches of the known world. This huge range of exotic combatants would have been a colourful circus sight to behold.

The following eight chapters of this book are devoted to giving a clear visual introduction to each of these warrior types.

SPARTAN HOPLITE

BATTLE OF THERMOPYLAE, 480 BC.

The Spartan King Leonidas and his royal bodyguard of 300 elite warriors fought for three days as part of a small allied Greek army at the Battle of Thermopylae.

The allied Greek force was a union of city-state men from all over Greece, all armed as heavy infantry spearmen known as hoplites. Clad in body armour, they wore bronze helmets and greaves, and carried the round Argive shield. The Greek force was made up of part-time soldiers, with merchants, farmers and craftsmen filling their ranks. All except for the 300 Spartans; their sole profession was warfare. The band of Greek men held their ground for three days at Thermopylae, holding back a huge Persian invasion force lead by King Xerxes.

THE DORY

The primary weapon in ancient Greek hoplite warfare was the spear or 'Dory' as it was known. The spear is believed to have been around 7 to 9 ft long, tipped with an iron leaf-shaped spearhead. At the bottom end was a metal counterweight butt-spike called a 'sauroter', which could be made from bronze or iron. This could be used as a backup if the iron head broke off in battle.

The spear would be used to thrust in an overarm action at the heads and bodies of their enemy. From behind their wall of shields, each warrior would jab and stab with downward thrusts as a unit, pushing and shoving against the opposition's own shield wall. As the unit of warriors (or 'phalanx') pushed forward, the fallen, wounded enemy would be trampled underfoot, then finished off by the rear ranks of the phalanx with heavy blows from their dories' butt-spikes.

The dory's slender shaft was made from Ash trees, a wood which was strong, light and readily available in the ancient Mediterranean. Making replacement shafts would have been something commonly seen in the armoury workshops of Greek cities.

Days before the battle, the Greek forces reinforced an old defensive wall known as the Phocian Wall. The old, stone wall spanned the marshy coastal pass at Thermopylae, from the waters of the Malian Gulf to the steep walls of Mount Kallidromos. The Greek plan was to funnel and hold the vast Persian army in this natural bottleneck. To Xerxes the narrow pass was a vital route that his massive force needed to push through in order to enter Greece.

The mountain geography and coastline enabled the small Greek force to face the immense Persian army on equal terms, without the danger of being enveloped. The narrow pass itself stripped Xerxes of his huge numerical advantage. Leonidas and the Greeks inflicted heavy losses on the Persian king's force.

Two days of hard fighting followed. On the morning of day three, Xerxes managed to outflank the Spartans and their fellow Greeks using information from a local Greek man who utterly betrayed his own countrymen for Persian gold. The traitor told Xerxes of the little-known Anopaia goat trail, a hidden path which crept around the mountains behind the pass at Thermopylae. The Persian king sent his elite Immortal warriors along the mountain trail to cut off the Greek warriors from reinforcement or escape. At this point in the battle it became clear to Leonidas that the Greek force had no hope of holding the pass. The Greek army was disbanded by the Spartan king and retreated for home to defend and ready their own cities for the imminent invasion. Leonidas, with his surviving Spartans plus a small band of Greek volunteers and their loyal servants, would defend the pass and cover the retreat of the withdrawing Greeks. This grim rearguard of stubborn Greek warriors formed the ranks of their phalanx formation and advanced forward over the wall into the pass. Taking the

fight to the Persians, the men of Greece committed to their last wild engagement.

When word spread to the allied camp that the Persians had taken the Anopaia path and would be outflanking the Greek force at any moment, a Spartan by the name of Eurytus called for his servant to dress him in his armour. Eurytus, not wanting to miss the action, or be forever shamed for not fighting with his Spartan brothers, made his way past the groups of retreating Greeks to the battle lines and joined the bloody melee. Eurytus had been blinded by severe eye infections.

In this last bitter fight, the Spartans rubbed salt deep into the Persians' wounds by killing members of Xerxes' own family.

Fury and wrath poured down on Xerxes' troops. Legend has it that so fierce and relentless was the Greek onslaught, that the Persian officers (knowing their king was watching) desperately whipped their own men forward onto the Greek spears. Leonidas himself, exhausted after slaying so many of his foe, fell from multiple wounds. A mad struggle raged for the dead Spartan's body as the Persians tried to take the fallen king's corpse as a trophy for Xerxes.

Knowing their time was finally up, the remaining Spartans withdrew to a small hill in the pass. The sun-baked hill would be the site of their last stand against the horde of surrounding Persian troops. With shattered spears and broken swords they fought on, with fists and teeth they raged, determined to drag more

Persians with them to the afterlife.

After viewing the gore-caked carpet of dead Immortals and smelling the stinking mounds of dead conscripts from all over his vast empire, the great king snapped. Enraged and frustrated at the insolent Greeks for refusing to submit to his rule, He ordered a storm of eastern arrows to end the fury of the Spartans' suicidal blood lust.

A vast cloud of arrows followed, blotting out the hot sun, allowing a moment or two for the last Spartans to fight in the shade. Volley after volley of arrows rained down on the last brave Greeks, bringing their valiant resistance to its end.

THE ARGIVE SHIELD

The main piece of Greek hoplite protective equipment was the large Argive shield, a wooden bowl-shaped shield made of willow, poplar or oak timber. Its diameter was around 80cm to 1m and had a depth of around 10cm. It could be faced with a very thin skin of bronze or in a hardened leather. On its inside a lining of fine leather or fabric could be glued in place onto its wooden core, or it could have attractive patterns and images painted on it.

The warrior would carry the Argive with his left arm, which fitted through a bronze support band called a 'porpax'. The porpax armband could have thick padded tubes of felt, leather or sheep fleece for added comfort. Around the porpax, close to the shield's outer rim, are a group of eight bronze rings or loops through which the cord hand grip or Antilabe was feed.

Some warriors chose to have a curtain of heavy fabric, leather or thick felt hung from the shield. This would help protect the lower legs from missile attacks from archers and slingers who would shower the

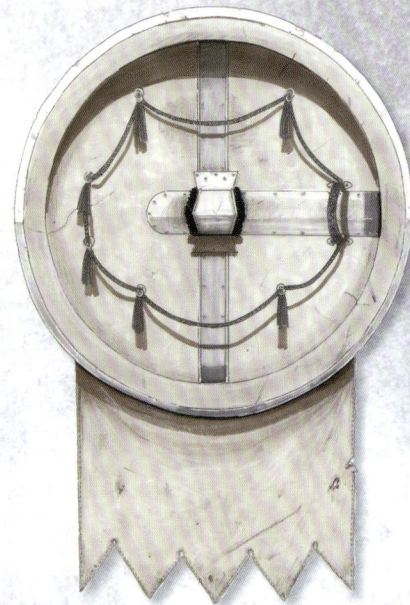

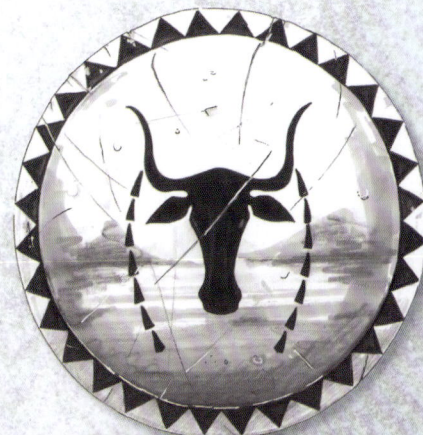

ABOVE: THE SPARTAN LAMBDA SHIELD SYMBOL.
BELOW: THE SHIELD SYMBOL USED BY THE
THEBANS WAS THE CLUB OF HERAKLES.

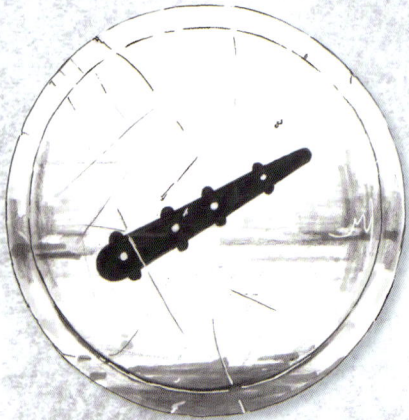

advancing phalanx with arrows and heavy lead shot before they engaged in direct combat.

Surviving examples of Argive shields from Olympia show very intricate porpax and antilabe bronze fittings and shield rim designs with complex patterns worked into them. Such fittings would have been expensive items, making a shield a valuable piece of property.

Such a costly item of kit would have been an important symbol of family honour, to lose it in battle was considered a terrible sin.

The Greek biographer Plutarch tells of a Spartan mother who on handing her boy his shield sternly told him to return 'either with it or on it'.

'On it' meant carried home injured or dead on the shield itself.

Greek vase paintings show a huge range of shield emblems, from all kinds of animal designs, religious symbols, bold patterns and even images of ships.

The purpose of such designs may have been a simple means of personal recognition, as the warriors' faces could not be easily seen from under the enclosed helmets. Family emblems, designs considered to be lucky or religious belief would no doubt influence the warrior's choice of motif. Plutarch again offers an insight into such choice of design when he tells of how a Spartan warrior commissioned a tiny insect to be painted on his shield. When asked why it was so small, the Spartan's reply was laced with dark humour, saying 'he would be so close to his enemy it would be very clear to see'.

As times changed, the Spartan military started to use a standardized uniform symbol on their shields. This was a lambda, the Greek letter L, standing for Lacedaemon (the state comprising Sparta and its territory).

The use of a city state emblem over individual designs is totally in keeping with the 'state first' military culture of Sparta. Its simple design, resembling an inverted 'V' was instantly recognizable from a distance. Soon other city-states adopted this state-emblem-only system. The Theban hoplites used the image of the club of Herakles, who was the city's patron god. The Mantineians painted their Argive shields with the trident of Poseidon, as he was their patron god.

LEFT: THE ARGIVE SHIELD'S CONCAVE INNER SIDE WITH ITS BRONZE PORPAX, ANTILABE HAND GRIP AND CORD SYSTEM. A PLATE OF BRONZE IS AFFIXED UNDER THE LEATHER LINING TO ADD PROTECTION TO THE AREA AROUND THE WARRIOR'S FOREARM.

CRIMSON CLOAKS AND TUNICS

The Spartans wore a simple crimson tunic called a chiton made of wool or linen under their armour. It was a rectangle of crimson-dyed cloth pinned at the shoulder and tied at the waist with some form of leather or fabric belt. The warlike colour of red suited the Spartans' mentality. Blood does not show up against red fabric in the same way as it stands out against other colours. A Spartan would not want his enemies to see him bleed, this would be a visual sign of weakness. This colour was adopted by later militaries from Alexander the Great's Macedonians, to Rome's legions and the regiments of the British Empire.

The tribon cloak worn by Spartan men was also crimson and of wool. It was worn wrapped close around the body. This thin garment offered little protection from the weather as the Spartan was expected to not need the luxury of warm comfort. The thinner the cloak, the tougher the man; the more worn out and threadbare, the better Spartan you were.

THE 300

Leonidas, knowing the battle for Thermopylae would be a fight to the death, picked 'Spartiates' (all fathers and true, full-citizen men) to accompany him. This was to make sure the family blood lines would live on after the father's death. Three hundred elite warriors made up his royal bodyguard or 'Hippeis' which he was allowed to take with him to Thermopylae. It is said that a strict religious festival barred him from taking a larger force, but it may have been that the five powerful Spartan 'ephoroi' (highly respected elders, who truly ruled the Spartan state) did not wish the whole Spartan army to be sent to fight so far north, as such a large military deployment would leave their home city-state open to attack from local enemies. Nevertheless, Leonidas marched to war singing to the sound of the Spartan pipes, fully aware of his fate.

BELOW: THE SPARTAN SHORT SWORD, AND THE XIPHOS SWORD PATTERN.

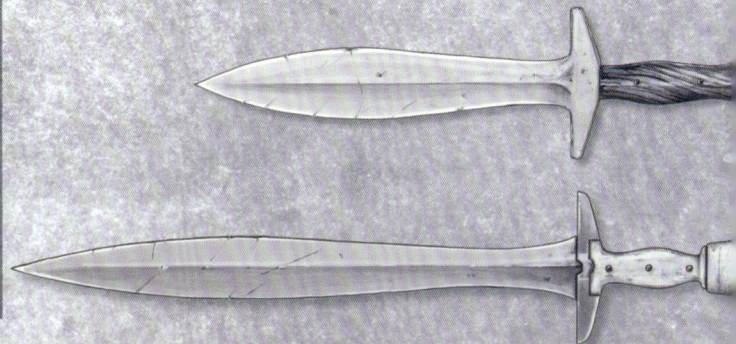

TYPES OF THE KOPIS SINGLE-EDGED CURVED PATTERN.

THE SWORD

The Spartan carries an iron-bladed, double-edged sword known as the xiphos. It is carried in a scabbard crafted from wood and skinned in dyed leather with fine oak and decorative bronze fittings used in its construction. A simple cord sling is used to carry the weapon close to the body while not in use.

At some point (after the Battle at Thermopylae in 480 BC) the swords used by the Spartans underwent a change in length. The basic blade patterns used by the rest of the classical Greek world, such as the curved kopis and the xiphos, fell from favour among the Spartan military. And shorter, dagger-size blades became popular as secondary weapons.

The Spartan short sword was an iron blade with a wooden or bone handle. It became a symbol of Spartan military power. It was mocked by other Greek warriors for its apparently inept size, but its short length gave an advantage to the user. When fighting in the mash of a tightly packed phalanx the longer traditional swords become unwieldy and harder to swing, such movements require a bit of space to build up a good amount of force.

A short blade can be thrust with greater ease with far less space needed to make a killing strike, jabbing and slashing at the enemies less-protected face, neck, arms and thighs. Its length also forces the user to commit to very close-quarter fighting and make far more aggressive sustained attacks. Being shorter also made it lighter and thus gave the warrior less of a burden to carry. Once a highly trained Spartan warrior has closed in on you to this degree your long spear is simply useless, and you are probably doomed.

No example of the short sword has survived, but it is estimated to have been around 30 to 40cm long; in comparison the other longer Greek swords where around 50 to 60cm long.

BODY ARMOUR

The Spartan hoplite wears a linen and leather composite cuirass, known as a linothorax. This style of body armour was becoming common amongst hoplite armies around this time and had replaced older, heavier bronze body armours. Being more flexible, lighter and cheaper to manufacture made it a far better armour all round. The linen was layered up, and perhaps laminated using some form of natural bonding agent, then stitched together up to twelve to sixteen layers thick and applied to the leather base. This offers great stopping power to arrows and cutting strikes as it absorbs and disperses the hit. The composite cuirass would not cook or burn the wearer like a bronze or iron cuirass while under the hot sun, nor would it chill the warrior during the snows of winter. This in turn would ease the physical strain on the warrior.

At its right underarm panel is a field of iron scales, each row overlapping the next. This right side of the body was most inviting to the thrust of an enemy's spear as it was not completely covered by the shield. The warrior's own right arm would have been raised, holding his spear in the fighting stance, thus exposing this underarm area.

A waistband of patterned leather covers the joint in the linen and leather panels. Bold Greek key designs and other geometric patterns were very much the fashion on this type of armour. A host of styles can be seen on Greek vase paintings.

The warrior's lower torso is covered by two layers of a split skirt of multi-layered linen and leather strips known as pteryges (meaning feathers in Greek). These pteryges flexed and opened with the warrior's movements while retaining a good protective coverage. The pteryges end around the groin area, guarding the soft guts of the warrior

LAYER UPON LAYER OF LINEN AND LEATHER MAKE UP THE TOUGH BASE STRUCTURE. WHILE THE OVERLAPING METAL SCALES ADD AN ATTRACTIVE, FLEXIBLE, PROTECTIVE SKIN.

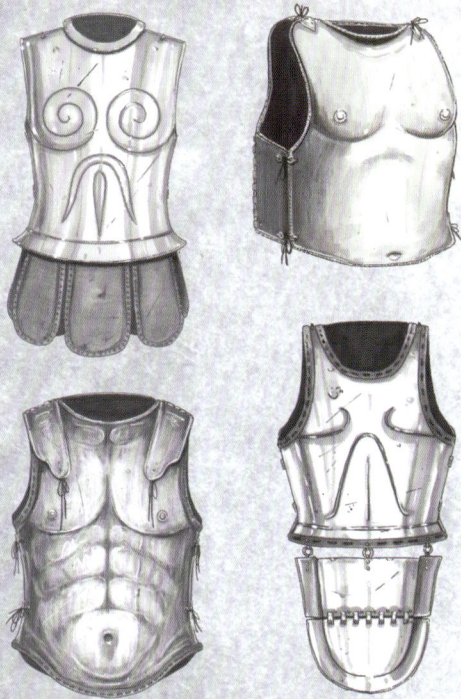

ABOVE: A RANGE OF BRONZE CUIRASS TYPES ALL DISPLAYING DEGREES OF ANATOMICAL STYLING.

GREAVES

The lower legs are protected by a set of bronze greaves. The Argive shield did not extend down past the mid-thigh, leaving the lower leg open to attack. This weak point had to be armoured so the development of the greave began. Simply fashioned to follow the muscular form of the lower leg from ankle to knee, the natural spring of the shaped bronze would hold the metal greave tightly clenched around the leg. They were tailored to fit the owner to near perfection and would have required a great deal of skill to construct. A soft, padded anklet helped stop the lower part of the greave from nipping and chaffing the ankles. Some greaves became very decorative and incredibly anatomical. Whether every citizen warrior in the phalanx wore greaves is not known. Ultimately the individual man's personal wealth would no doubt dictate this.

Other greave designs like the famous Thracian Vratsa and Agighiol greaves were fantastical, featuring zoomorphic imagery and the faces of goddesses incorporated into the designs. These high-status royal greaves (more works of art then war gear) were created by gilding, hammering, chiseling and casting the metals.

from low, stabbing blows. Pteryges could also be made from heavy, thick leather, leather with overlapping metal scales applied, or multiple layers of overlapping wool strips.

The thorax's yoke is covered with decorated bronze plates featuring eight-rayed Argead star and floral motifs, popular designs from the Classical age to the Hellenistic period. Oiled leather thongs tie the yoke down onto a central boss on the mid-chest. This overlap of yoke and chest panel doubles the protection to an area most likely to take hits from downward spear thrust, or arrow strikes.

At this time the city-states of ancient Greece did not equip their warriors with armour, so the personal wealth of the individual warrior would dictate the materials used in the construction of his body armour. A less wealthy man may have worn a simple leather cuirass of the same cut known as a spolas, while far-grander composite armours made from richly dyed linens, tooled leathers and covered in bronze, iron plates and scales would be available to the richer members of a Greek army. So, a hoplite force's appearance would have been a jumble of styles and colour due to the irregular personal economics of its citizen warriors.

HELMETS

The most famous helmet of the Ancient world was perhaps the Corinthian helmet. It was made of a bronze sheet hammered into its iconic shape by the expert armourers of their age. It enclosed the head of the wearer completely except for its stylized eyes and pointed nasal guard, from which the central front slit opening runs. Either side of this opening are the fixed cheek guards which flair into an elegant, pointing slope, protecting the wearer's bare neck. The Corinthian model was the result of a gradual trial-and-error process from the Archaic period onwards, its lines becoming more graceful as the type evolved. Its shape was linked to the style of fighting its wearer was engaged in, this was close-quarter spear fighting from behind a wall of shields. In this style of combat, the face was exposed to the jabbing and thrusting of the opponent's spear. The eyes, nose and as much of the front of the wearer's head as possible needed to be protected, while still allowing the warrior to see and breath easily. Later models began to have less covering around the ears to allow for better hearing, which was becoming more important as the development of complex battle movements and orders needed to be undertaken and communicated.

Another helmet type was the open-faced Illyrian.

THE CORINTHIAN HELMET'S EVOLUTION, FROM THE BASIC EARLY 7TH CENTURY BC PATTERN (HELMET 1) TO ITS FINAL GRACEFUL SHAPE AROUND 500 BC (HELMET 5). THE LATER CORINTHIANS WERE THE BASIS FOR THE CHANGE TO THE CHALCIDIAN AND THE ATTIC PATTERNS. BOTH TYPES COULD SPORT FIXED OR HINGED CHEEK GUARDS.

The Illyrian helmet had a raised channel running down its crown and shared the flared back neckline of the Corinthian. As with the Corinthian, the later models of the Illyrian opened up around the ear. The wearer of an Illyrian must have chosen this helmet as he preferred the benefits of free vision and cooler ventilation to the enclosed protection of the Corinthian, a hard choice to make when battling in the scorching months of a Mediterranean summer.

Many images from pottery of the period show warriors sporting tall crests sitting on top of their helms, resembling the manes of horses. These crests flow upwards from boxes normally decorated with complex geometric patterns. What these crest boxes were made from is unclear, but it would have to be light and strong, perhaps a stiffened leather or a light wood.

Horsehair, knotted grass fibre, feathers, and stiff-cut leather could have been used to create these impressive helmet toppers. If the warriors wore new, freshly made crests for every set battle is unclear, but a hoplite, like any soldier, would want to look good when facing his foe. These crests could be used for personal identity or a mark of rank. They could be coloured to a multitude of patterns using the dyes and paints of the age.

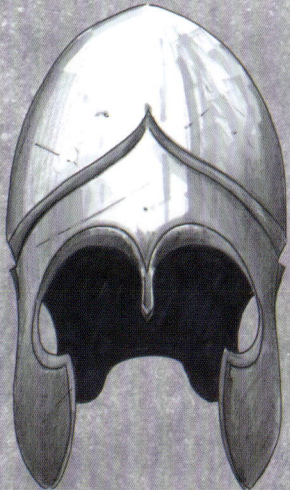

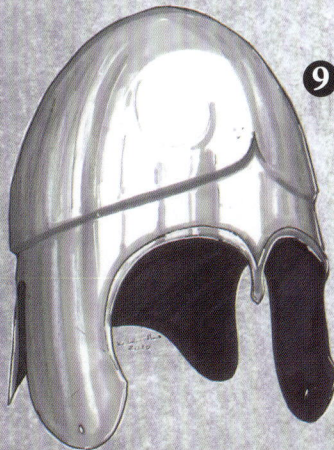

(HELMET 7) THE ATTIC TYPE HAD LITTLE OR NO NOSE GUARD, AND HINGED CHEEK GUARDS. (HELMETS 8, 9, 10) THE CHALCIDIAN TYPE. (HELMET 6) THE ILLYRIAN HELMET PATTERN, A FAR MORE SEVERE SHAPE THAN THE SLEEK CORINTHIAN.

SPARTAN

Kicking and screaming I entered this world, kicking and screaming is how I will leave it with rock in hand atop this mound of their smashed dead!

DAMAGED BEYOND USE, THE WARRIOR HAS FINALLY HAD TO DISCARD HIS BATTERED SHIELD. NOT WANTING TO BE ROBBED OF A GLORIOUS DEATH BY SOME EASTERN ARCHER, HE DESCENDS INTO A FINAL WILD AND DESPERATE BRAWL WITH XERXES' OWN IMMORTALS. PIERCED BY ARROWS AND WEAPONLESS, ARMED ONLY WITH RED MIST AND ROCK.

MACEDONIAN PHALANGITE

THE BATTLE OF ISSUS, 333 BC.

This man is a veteran phalangite of Alexander the Great's long march of conquest into and beyond the Persian Empire. He has fought his way across the known world, killed countless numbers of enemies, and survived wounds and illness for his young king.

He is one of thousands of Macedonians who have been trained and drilled in the deadly art of phalanx warfare. His tools, the 18ft sarissa pike and the 2ft diameter bronze-faced pelta shield seem somewhat unwieldy, but when added to the massed ranks of his identically armed countrymen they became an impenetrable spiked wall of moving death, which their enemy could do little to counter.

Born in the tough highlands of Macedonia, he had a harsh and humble peasant life guarding flocks of goats and sheep from predators and robbers. This rough, tough life made him good building material for Alexander's growing national army. Eager to bring fortune and maybe fame home once the young king was done smashing the Persians, he would see wonders, hardship and brute carnage long before his return to Macedonia.

Military drill was key to his training and to King Alexander's success; it would be drummed into him to become second nature. His ability to march at speed while carrying equipment and rations for prolonged periods in all weathers, along with a controlled aggression, fierce loyalty and discipline, made him the perfect soldier.

THE BATTLE OF ISSUS

The Battle of Issus was a key victory for Alexander the Great, who, as was his style, lead his men from the front. It was Alexander and his own elite cavalry (the Companion cavalry) who won the day for the Macedonians. Alexander's infantry in the centre of the battle line became at risk of being crushed by the overwhelming amount of Persian and Greek mercenary infantry fighting for the Persian King Darius. Darius' centre force had engaged the Macedonian phalanx infantry on the coastal plain around the River Pinarus (modern day Turkey). The rough terrain around the river and the rain of Persian arrows and sling shot caused the phalanx formations to break up as they marched forward over the broken ground; this weakened its fighting cohesion as the two forces slammed together in a mighty clash. The struggle was intense and brutal with huge loses to each side.

But the superior discipline and training of Alexander's infantry meant they managed to fight and hold their line against a far-larger force on unfavourable ground.

Alexander (after crushing his first targets on the Persian army's left flank), swung around with the Companion cavalry and his fast moving Hypaspists (warriors armed in the hoplite manner) to strike at the heart of Darius' main fighting force which was hammering away at the Macedonian phalanx. Alexander's cavalry charge was so effective it utterly smashed the Persian lines and forced King Darius to flee from battle.

Once Darius fled, chaos followed and his army crumbled. The men of the Macedonian phalanx, now able to advance and pursue their fleeing enemy, killed thousands of men as they worked their way forward into the retreating mass of the Persian horde.

It is said that an army loses more men in such disordered retreats than in the battle itself.

THE MACEDONIAN PHALANX

The Macedonian phalanx was a formation of fighting men formed up into ranks and files. One file was made up of 16 men and known as a lochos; 8 lochoi made a taxis (128 men); 2 taxeis made the syntagma (256 men); and 2 syntagamas formed the pentecosiarchia, a unit of 512 men in total.

The first five rows of men (or front-rankers) would include the more battle-hardened men. They would advance with the long sarissa lowered for the attack held firm with both hands, the relentless drive of this mass of spearpoints would pin and trap the enemy while Alexander and his Companion cavalry swept in from the flanks to hammer home a lightning attack. If an enemy made it past the stabbing thrusts of the first sarissa he would find four more eager spearheads awaiting, making it a very hard task to close in on the Macedonian men.

ABOVE, THE BASIC SYNTAGMA UNIT WAS 256 MEN STRONG. BELOW, TWO SYNTAGMAS MADE THE TERRIFYING 512-STRONG PENTACOSIARCHIA. MULTIPLE PENTACOSIARCHIA FORMATIONS WOULD MAKE UP THE MACEDONIAN BATTLE LINE.

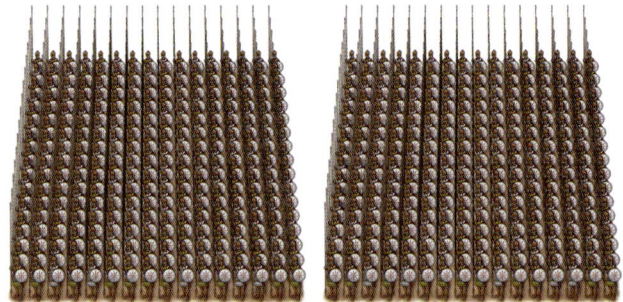

THE GREAVES

The soldier wears a pair of iron greaves taken from a dead Greek mercenary in the aftermath of an earlier battle. They protect the vulnerable exposed lower legs. Behind the iron is a dense layer of felt sandwiched under a goatskin lining, this would cushion against any blow to the leg and make for a comfortable fit. Two straps and buckles aid in keeping the greave on the leg while on the march and preventing fallen enemies from ripping them off as they are trampled underfoot. The edge of the iron was drilled to allow the stitching of a leather binding.

THE SARISSA

The primary weapon of the phalangite was the sarissa spear (or pike) from 16ft to 18 ft long and comprised of two lengths of wooden shaft. One shaft was tipped with the iron spearhead, the other with the iron or bronze butt-spike and they were connected by an iron tube which the two shafts would slot into to become the full length. The butt-spike acted as a counterweight for balance as the assembled weapon was not easy to hold when its weight was at the spearhead end. It is unlikely this butt-spike could be used as a backup weapon if the spear point was damaged, as the heavier butt end itself would need its own counterweight to stop it dropping. Also, the space needed to move the butt end to face the enemy without clashing against his fellow countrymen's sarissa would not be available in the tightly formed phalanx.

This man's state-supplied sarissa has a fresh replacement spearhead shaft. On the march the sarissa could be broken down into its two shorter parts for easier transport. A simple leather carrier bag with a looped handle is used by this man while on the march; the two shafts sit cradled side by side while a leather thong lashes the spearhead end to the other shaft.

A draw back to the sarissa was if an enemy (or his horse) wearing no armour were foolish enough (or blinded by the dense dust clouds of battle) to engage the phalangites in a mad frontal charge he would risk completely impaling himself upon the spear points of the sarissa. While killing the enemy it would also render the long spear completely useless and the phalangite would have no choice but to discard it and draw his sword. Just one freaked-out horse stuck on three or four sarissa tips, rolling and kicking wildly, could completely break the first few ranks' strength. This in turn would weaken the phalanx's ordered wall of spears and cause a gap to appear; these gaps would then allow a determined second wave of enemy to push into the Macedonian ranks.

The men of the phalanx must have liked a damp, dustless battlefield, allowing the enemy the full terrifying sight of their ordered advance. The sight alone of a Macedonian sarissa wall would cause most enemy charges to stall with fear.

THE SHIELD

The pelta shield was a smaller, much-lighter and less-domed shield than the hoplite Argive shield. Made of poplar or willow, it measured around 64cm in diameter and had a thin, bronze facing. A group of leather straps are fitted to the inside for the arm and hand to fit and grip against. No bronze porpax has been fitted to the shallow-domed shield as it would make the slinging of the shield uncomfortable during the long marches to battle. A bronze porpax would also add weight to the warrior's already burdened left arm. A leather sling is fitted to allow the weight of the shield to be shared between the arm, neck and shoulder, as both arms are busy carrying the long, heavy sarissa spear. It has a narrow ring of red-dyed leather pinned to the inner rim to cover the jagged bronze folded darts of the shield's facing. On the inner side of the shield, under a simple leather porpax-type arm loop sits a thick pad of felt, fitted into a linen cover. This would help with comfort and also reduce the force of heavy impacts on the warrior's arm.

Its bronze face is painted white with a simple design of a red, eight-rayed star applied to its centre. This may have been a unit emblem. Eight-rayed stars were a common motif on shields and armour. Some bronze facings included complex geometric patterns and even figurative images tooled into the thin, metal skin. These complex patterned shields must have been expensive to manufacture and thus must have been used by elite units or men of note and wealth. Lesser units may well have carried pelta shields covered in a skin of hardened leather with no bronze facing at all.

POLISHED BRONZE-FACED PELTA SHIELDS WITH COMPLEX DESIGNS TOOLED INTO THE THIN, METAL SKIN.

THE PILOS HELMET

This bronze conical helmet copies the style of a popular hat known as the pilos which was made of felt. It is made of bronze and has bronze cheek guards. It is lined with a thick felt padded liner.

Its shape made for an easy manufacture which would make it popular as it was far cheaper to equip large groups of men, perfect when the state was paying.

The conical shape would deflect downward hits from missile weapons, like arrows and heavy sling shot which would rain down upon the advancing phalanx.

This phalangite has over his time in service customized the basic helmet by adding cheek guards. Being in the front row of a phalanx, any upgrades to armour protection would be very wise and desirable.

It has been painted blue to aid unit recognition on the field. The two white horsehair plumes are a mark of rank, that of a more senior man of the phalanx, perhaps a file-leader.

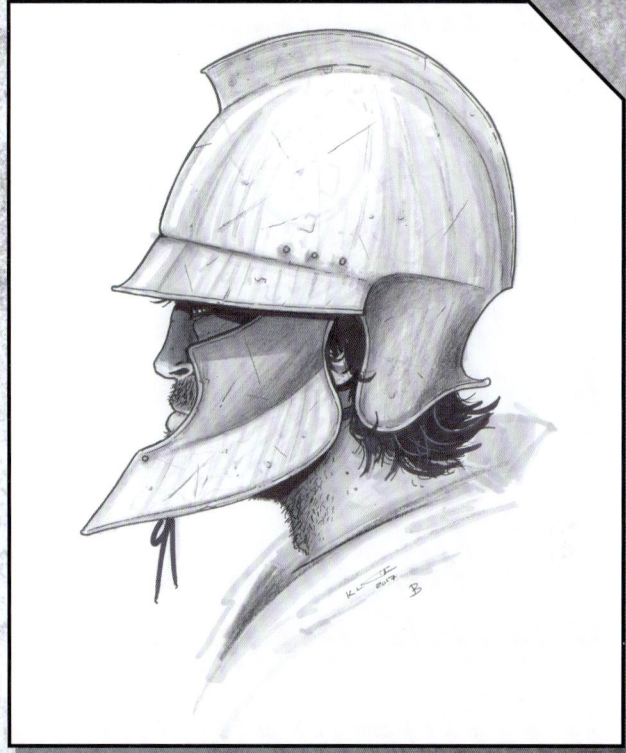

THE PILOS (A), AND TWO TYPES OF THRACIAN STYLE HELMET. THESE WOULD BE COMMONLY SEEN AMONG THE RANK AND FILE OF THE PHALANX.

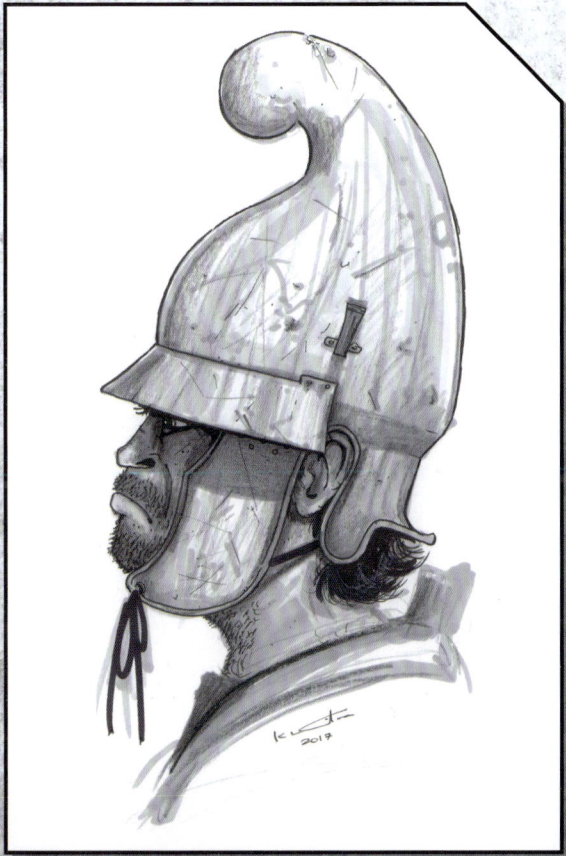

A

MACEDONIAN PHALANGITE

Ahead of us on the far bank, a great boiling mass of Persians and paid Greek traitors came into view. Then the storm began, their arrows and lead shot rained down heavily as we advanced down into the cold river. Men crashed into the water in hellish agony all around me as Persian arrows pierced flesh and bone. A lead shot slammed onto my shield's bronze face, making a loud hollow clang, its force smashed the shield up into my jaw and lip, injecting the iron taste of blood into my mouth.

Some of the boys to my right were wading waist-deep across the cloudy river now. My cousin on my left was up to his chest when he took a glancing lead shot hit to his helmet. Its strike snapped his head back violently and he fell under the murky flow of water, remerging moments later, only to lose his footing on the loose pebble riverbed, sending him under again, face first. He came up gasping for air, cursing the gods with true Macedonian flair.

THE LINOTHORAX

The phalangite wears a state-issued linothorax, a basic body armour which he has upgraded with a heavy lamellar bronze yoke made from overlapping plates of bronze stitched to a leather base.

Top layers of yellow and purple-dyed cloth are added to the man's armour as a means of unit identification; he has also personalized his suit by adding a bronze lion-head disc for decoration.

The body armour, like the earlier hoplite's thorax, is made up of multiple layers of linen and leather bonded and stitched together and has similar protective properties to a modern flak jacket. Capable of stopping and softening impacts from pointed weapons, its composite construction made it a very tough and durable peace of war gear. The pteryges (skirt) of this armour has a considerably longer base skirt, this is due to the pelta shield having a lesser diameter and exposing a greater area of leg and thigh to attack. This man replaced a damaged shorter base set of pteryges with a new, longer, uncoloured linen set. They have been retro-fitted in camp at one of the army's baggage-train workshops between the long treks to battle.

It is not high-end armour like that worn by the nobles and wealthy officers, but a mass-produced model made for the Macedonian army's campaign into the Persian Empire.

Well-worn and under constant maintenance and repair, a piece of state-owned armour would have been worn by a number of men, passed from dead man to living. Cheaper it may have been, but such a piece of equipment would become valuable to the army whose supply lines could stretch hundreds of miles and new suits may not have been available for months or years.

Any army operating under such conditions would simply re-issue armour until it was completely unserviceable; retro-fitting and customizing equipment at the wearer's expense will have been (as is today) a practice every soldier would be accustomed to.

Alexander ordered the burning of the old armour in India (this could only have happened upon the delivery of fresh linothorax) so one can assume the old linen sets would have been very unpleasant to wear after years of sweat, blood and grime. This, on top of the humid Indian weather, must have left them threadbare and smelly.

At his waist the warrior wears a simple leather belt to help hold the armour and to carry his coin pouch. He carries some of his personal fortune of pay and plunder with him as he does not wish to lose it all should the baggage train be captured.

THE SWORD

The secondary weapon, and last resort should the sarissa become completely unusable, was the sword. This soldier uses the kopis, a single-edged, curved, iron blade, ideal for hacking at the enemy. This pattern was widespread across the classical and Hellenistic world. It also makes a good multi-purpose tool as well as a weapon. It is a state-issued, basic, mass-produced weapon and is carried in a simple leather sheath.

MACEDONIAN COMPANION CAVALARYMAN

BATTLE OF GAUGAMELA, 331 BC.

This trooper of the Macedonian Companion cavalry is in the thick of combat at a place known by the local men as Gaugamela. Following his King Alexander, he and his fellow Macedonian horsemen punched a hole deep into the very heart of the Persian army lines with the intention of killing its high commanders and the Persian King Darius himself.

Darius was so shocked by Alexander's direct and determined effort to kill him that he turned and ran from the dusty battlefield in fear of his life, totally abandoning the men of his huge Persian army and handing Alexander victory once more.

The veteran Companion trooper had served King Philip II before his murder in 336 BC and continued to serve his homeland's royal family in Asia with Philips' son Alexander. He had been with Philip during his bloody campaign against the northern tribes of Thrace and had seen victory at the Battle of Chaeronea in 338 BC. Here at Chaeronea, he and his fellow Macedonian warriors aided King Philip in crushing the Thebans and Athenians into submission. This victory forced an unhappy union between the city-states of Greece and Macedonia in what was known as the League of Corinth.

He followed his new king into Asia and fought hard against the Persians at the bloody battles of Granicus and Issus. Then with Alexander he marched south into the ancient and wonderful kingdom of Egypt. Here among the exotic grand temples he witnessed Alexander's crowning as pharaoh of all Egypt.

To his list of adventures, he now adds Gaugamela.

COMPANION CAVALRY

The Companion cavalry regiment or 'Hetairoi' was the elite force of horsemen Alexander the Great took with him into Persia to smash Darius' Persian empire. All were favoured Macedonian men and most loyal to their young king.

It is said that the Macedonian infantry phalanx was Alexander's anvil, and the Companion cavalry were his hammer, a fast and heavy hitting unit of highly trained and disciplined troopers drawn from the rich families of the Macedonian ruling classes.

These men could afford all the trappings required for mounted combat. To join this elite force would bring great prestige and honour to their families back home, while also raising their social status and influence at court.

Riding in a triangular wedge formation and armed with the long cavalry spear, the trooper and his fellow countrymen would present a bristling wedge of thunderous momentum, ploughing into and shattering enemy lines through sheer momentum and discipline.

The long lance or xyston is believed to have had a spear head at each end of its shaft. The heavy impact on the enemy could break its long shaft in two. By having a spear point at each end, the trooper could bring the remaining usable spear head into use and continue the fight. Not an easy manoeuvre when riding in close formation among raging enemy troops. To simply drop a shattered xyston could also present a real danger to the horses and men behind, impaling or tripping your comrade's mount could create a catastrophic pile up, ending an attack. So good training and a vice-like grip would have been key.

THE MACEDONIAN CAVALRY WEDGE FORMATION.

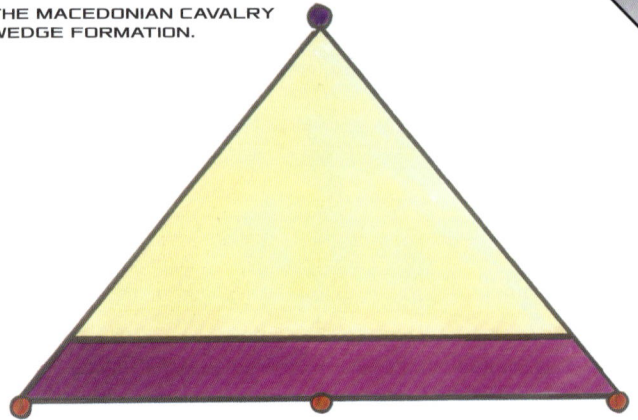

An officer is stationed at the tip of each point of the triangle wedge formation, with a fourth placed in the centre of the rear rank to keep order and control. The wedge was around 50 riders strong, 4 such fighting wedges making up a Macedonian cavalry squadron of 200 men and horses. This squadron was commanded by a high-ranking officer known as an ilarch.

Commander = Purple
Officer = Red
Cavalry Troopers = Yellow and Purple

THE KAUSIA HAT

This simple beret-like hat is made of clean, white wool felt and was a typical piece of Macedonian national clothing. This style can be seen in coin designs from the fourth and third centuries BC featuring the Macedonian kings of old. A similar style hat is worn in Afghanistan today and could well have its origins in the Macedonian kausia. Alexander and his Macedonian generals colonized this part of the Persian empire with Greek and Macedonian veterans who would have worn such hats. When not wearing their heavy bronze and iron helmets, the Macedonian men of Alexander's army would have worn this practical hat while at work around camp, and while on the march. Its shape would keep the burning sun off during the hot summers, and its wool felt kept the head warm and dry in the winter months.

JEWELLERY

The trooper wears around his neck a scarab-shaped pendant made from dark blue faience. This exotic and most un-Greek piece was bought in Egypt as a memento to mark the young King Alexander of Macedonia being crowned pharaoh of all Egypt. It has so far brought the owner good luck.

THE BOEOTIAN HELMET

The trooper wears a Boeotian helmet made of bronze. This style of helmet was favoured by horsemen of the period. This may have been due to its open-faced design, which allowed excellent vision and hearing. Its bronze folds fall to protect the face from slashing attacks. The helmet's exaggerated peak protects the wearer's face and eyes from the sun's glare and the rain's blinding effects while also shielding the head from downward strikes from missile weapons.

Atop the helmet's conical bowl sits a mount for the topknot of white horsehair. This is a mark of rank. Such a horsehair crest is seen in the Roman mosaic from Pompeii which depicts Alexander the Great and a member of his cavalry mid-battle. A cord of purple is laced through the helmets small fitting apertures on each side. The cord then ties under the chin to secure the costly helmet to its owner's head.

A near-perfect Boeotian-style helmet was found in the muddy bed of the River Tigris, after being hidden and undisturbed for over two thousand years.

Fording a river is a difficult task, and a necessity for an army on the march. An army on a long campaign like Alexander the Great's, would make multiple river crossings, each with its own unique problems and dangers. Wearing heavy armour, while shifting equipment and awkward baggage adds an extra degree of risk to this already tricky task.

The Roman historian Curtius wrote about Alexander crossing the River Tigris. He wrote that the river at its deepest point was up to the Macedonian horses' necks, and that the river had a strong flow.

Large formations of disciplined troops soon break into disordered, strung out clusters, struggling against the river's flow, with cold water up to and above the waist, all the while treading on a loose, uneven and slippery riverbed. Men, equipment and pack animals would be lost to the river in the struggle. The Tigris Boeotian helmet may well have been lost in such a crossing by one of Alexander's Companion troopers who crossed the water on horseback, but the fate of its owner will never be known.

The Tigris helmet can be seen at the Ashmolean museum in Oxford, England.

THE XYSTON SPEAR

The long xyston spear was made of wood and was said to have two iron spear heads at each end and was longer than the typical hoplite's dory spear. Even-longer sarissa-type cavalry lances are known to have also been used and required two hands to wield. This would require a very skilled rider and a well-trained and trusted horse.

TUNIC

An expensive, purple, long-sleeved tunic of a fine wool and linen mix is worn. This is again a sign of his favoured elite status. It is worn belted at the waist with a sash. Long sleeves seem to have been the fashion during this period. The earlier classical periods saw simple rectangular tunics made from one piece of cloth being worn. This new style would require more fabric, and more costly colour. This would end with a degree of left-over cloth from the cutting of the narrow sleeves, a costly loss that only a king or wealthy family could afford.

CLOAK

This style of cloak was a distinctive piece of Macedonian clothing. Its cut was a quarter circle of yellow wool with a purple border at its bottom edge. This simple border detail shows this man to be a member of the Companion cavalry. The use of purple and yellow (the royal colour dyes) identifies the special importance this unit had to their King Alexander, as no other unit would be awarded such an expensive and colourful piece of uniform.

A disc-shaped bronze cloak brooch in the form of a gorgon's head holds the wool garment in place.

THE SWORD

The trooper carries an iron xiphos sword with a solid bronze handgrip as his secondary weapon. The double-edged blade is carried in its wooden scabbard, which has been covered with dyed red leather. It hangs close to the body via a leather strap system over the shoulder. This strap is decorated with small bronze discs and the leather has a stamped design pressed onto its surface. At its end the scabbard has a lion-shaped chape, again in bronze.

SHIELD

Unlike the Thracian, Scythian and Persian horsemen, the Macedonian and Greek cavalry units of the fourth century BC did not yet employ shields in combat. Later generations of Greek and Thracian cavalry did use large round and oval shields alongside spears shorter than the xyston.

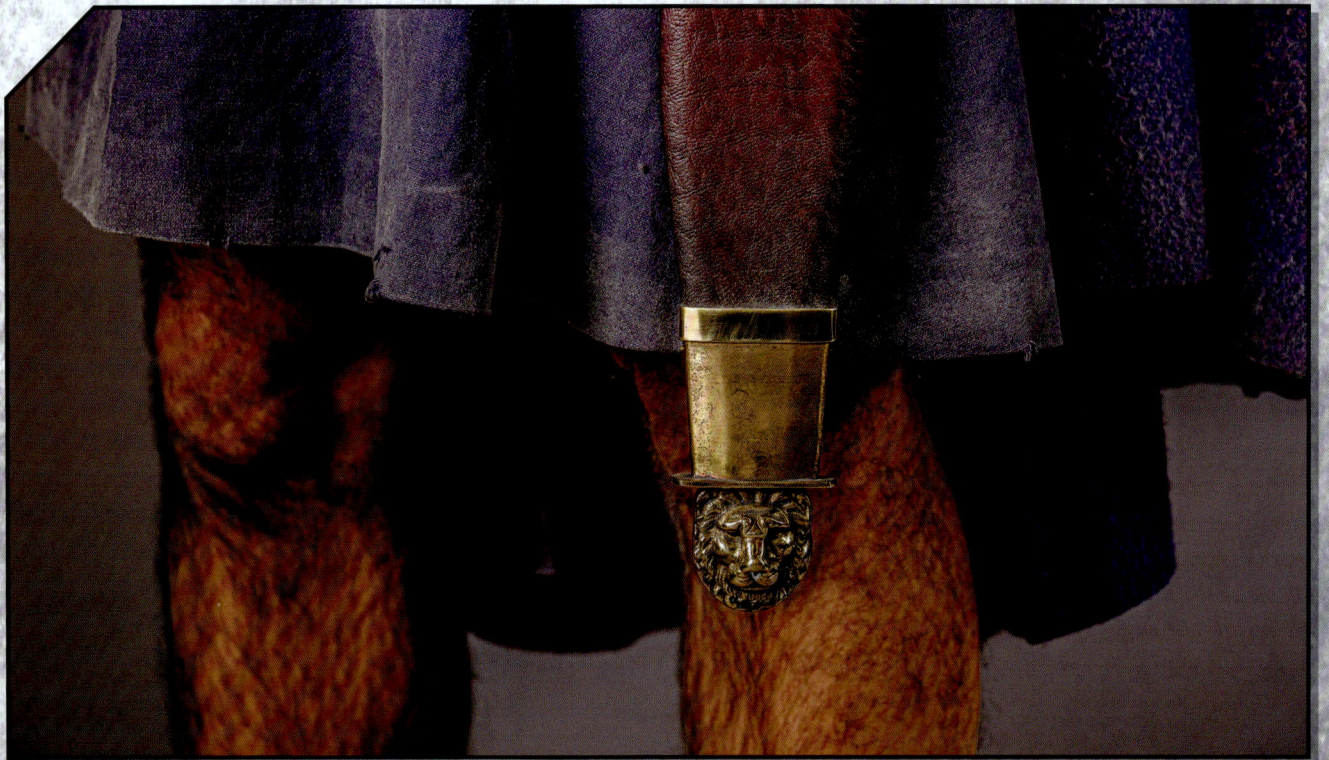

SCARF

The thick, dirty clouds of dust kicked up while riding or marching en masse can be both blinding and suffocating. This trooper has chosen to wear a scarf of yellow Indian cotton to stop the choking effects of the fine dust. A fit of coughing or heavy sneezes could cause a loss of control and render a warrior vulnerable to attack during the fast fighting of cavalry combat. The yellow cloth scarf was bought at one of the many markets supplied to Alexander's army on the road east.

ARMOUR

The warrior wears a cuirass made of bronze, crafted to mimic the muscle shapes of the male torso. Front and back plates are fastened at the sides and at the shoulders with a system of leather lacing. The leather cordage is looped and bowed through rings of bronze that are attached to the two metal plates. This allows a small degree of movement between the chest and back plates, giving the trooper the ability to pull the two plates closer to his body, or to slacken it at his waist. The shoulders are covered with a set of linen and leather-based shoulder guards, with each having a row of layered linen pteryges hanging from each to protect the upper arms.

At the bottom of the muscle cuirass hangs a full skirt of pteryges again fabricated in leather and linen which overlap to protect the trooper's abdomen without restricting movement of his hips. At his midrift, a sash of boldly patterned purple wool is tied in a bow to help hold the heavy bronze plates snugly in place while riding. Other types of bronze cuirasses show that a system of hinges and pins could be used to hold a cuirass's two plates as one. This is done by matching up the two bronze plates and their hinge tubes neatly together, then a pin is inserted into the aligned hinge tubes. This would affectively lock the metal chest and back plates together rigidly. This allows no movement to the wearer but does add solidity to the cuirass's form.

The rider wears no greaves on his legs; this may have been to keep the weight down, which would ease the strain on the horse and allow greater endurance during battle.

The riders on the Alexander the Great sarcophagus are shown wearing no armour at all. Alexander the Great himself was said to have gone into battle unarmoured more than once – a very risky tactical decision when your enemy employed massed ranks of skilled archers.

COMPANION CAVALRY TROOPER

The horses kicked up great clouds of dust and muck, and the roasting wind swirled it all around us, choking and blinding us all. For a moment as we galloped forward I caught sight of Alexander, his helmet dazzled through the blinding dust. His head was turned facing the Persian battle lines, eyes locked on the barbarian king like a hawk waiting for the perfect moment to dive on its prey. And dive he did, right for the heart of the vast Persian horde, right for the throat of King Darius himself!

PAEONIAN LIGHT CAVALRY

CROSSING THE RIVER TIGRIS, GAUGAMELA, 331 BC.

GAUGAMELA 331 BC

This Paeonian royal bodyguard would ride at the head of a contingent of auxiliary light cavalry, commanded by prince Ariston.

Unlike his fellow light Paeonian riders, this wealthy nobleman could afford to have one or two fresh horses in reserve to spread the burden of his armour – a luxury enjoyed only by royalty and the favoured warrior elite. He is armed in the Thracian manner.

HELMET

Upon his head the Paeonian bodyguard wears a Thracian helmet (or Phrygian helmet), made of iron. Like other helmets of the time it mimics a style of popular hat. Its copper-alloy, hinged cheek guards flare out to protect the throat from upward spear thrusts and a bronze visor has been later added to shield the eyes from the sun's glare and from attack.

On top of the tall helmet sits a crest of stiff, lightweight leather affixed in a patterned wooden box. This painted leather crest is a lighter, more durable alternative to horsehair plumes, which can sag over time.

His helmet has been painted purple (a royal colour) due to him being a member of Ariston's personal bodyguard unit. The two eagle feathers are a badge of rank.

Inside the helmet is a wool felt liner; this would soften any hits to the head and would also make a snug and comfortable fit while riding.

The Thracians and their neighbouring cousins are known to have worn helmets of all manner of Greek styles alongside the Phrygian, from the Corinthian, Chalcidian, and Boeotian helmets to the Attic type. Access to such headgear was easy through trade and private commission for the very wealthy, and through battle plunder when opportunity allowed.

BODY ARMOUR

The nobleman wears an iron scale armour designed perfectly for the use of a mounted cavalryman. Long pteryges (or skirt flaps) at the sides to guard the thighs and much-shorter flaps at the back and front made it a more practical armour for such seated fighting.

His sword is slung under the longer left thigh pteryges as the weight of the scales would help stop the weapon bouncing around while riding at speed. The yoke is again cut for purpose, the right side being cut in a staggered pattern to allow full free movement of the weapon-arm's downward swing of a sword or the arching launch of a javelin. Sacrificing defensive protection for the freedom of offensive movement was clearly a fair trade to this man. The left side is longer as this arm would be holding the horse's reins. The iron scales are stitched to a pliable leather backing in a way that each scale overlaps the next, effectively doubling the thickness of the metal scales while retaining its full flexibility.

This warrior's body armour is based on a suit from the Bulgarian state museum in Sofia. It was from the Royal Thracian burial mound of Golyamata Mogila and belonged to a warrior of great wealth.

PRINCE ARISTON

The Greek biographer Plutarch wrote about the Paeonian Prince Ariston and a daring defensive action he led.

A short while before the battle at Gaugamela, as Alexander the Great's forces approached the battle ground, a large skirmish took place on the banks of the nearby River Tigris. A large body of Persian horsemen, numbering around 1,000, had attacked the Macedonian forces crossing the river. According to Plutarch, Alexander, who had crossed the river on foot, ordered Prince Ariston and his Paeonian auxiliary light cavalry to protect the horribly exposed Macedonian troops fording the river.

Upon the banks of the Tigris, Ariston engaged the Persian cavalry commander Satropates in fierce personal combat. The prince's iron spearhead found its mark deep in the neck of Satropates. The Persian was violently unseated from his fine horse, mortally wounded and unable to escape the prince. The Persian nobleman was quickly ended by Ariston who promptly removed the dead commander's head from his body.

The Macedonian and allied Greek troops awaiting their turn to cross the Tigris had front-row seats to this extremely violent clash between the two commanders. They yelled and cheered their support for Ariston from across the flowing river. The Paeonian prince, filled with pride and swagger, hurried his fresh, grisly trophy to Alexander, tossing the prized Persian's head at the young king's feet.

Ariston's fearless attitude, loyalty, skill at arms, and leadership of his light cavalry left Alexander impressed. The Peaonian and his men had proven to be of great value that day.

The swift deployment of Ariston and his fast light cavalry against Satropates and the 1,000 Persian horsemen saved the troops fording the river. If it had not been for the bloodlust of the Paeonian and his men, the Persian forces may well have gained the upper hand. This would have brought disaster to Alexander on the banks of the River Tigris before the battle at Gaugamela had even been fought.

WEAPONS

The Paeonian and Thracian riders' primary weapons were a clutch of iron-tipped javelins (short throwing spears) which could double as short lances if needed. When launching the javelin from horseback at full tilt, the forward momentum of the horse multiplies the energy released by the rider at the moment of launch, sending the javelin forth with incredible speed and force. To leave the battlefield alive after taking a javelin hit would be a rare thing.

The warrior also carries the popular double-edged iron xiphos sword as his secondary weapon. Both javelin and xiphos are ideal killing tools for a light cavalryman.

A longer lance known as the xyston could also be carried, like the type used by the heavier Macedonian cavalry. Alexander the Great issued his own royal prodromoi ('frontrunners') light cavalry with the longer xyston in place of their javelins.

FOURTH CENTURY BC BRONZE CHALCIDIC HELMET WITH THREE-HEADED HYDRA DECORATION, FROM BULGARIA'S GOLYAMATA MOGILA BURIAL TUMULUS (ANCIENT THRACE). THIS HELMET HAD TRACES OF A LAMB'S-WOOL LINING CAP WHICH HAD BEEN DYED PURPLE STILL ATTACHED TO THE INNER DOME. THE HELMET IS BELIEVED TO HAVE BELONGED TO A THRACIAN PRINCE OF THE ODRYSIAN KINGDOM.

THE PAEONIAN

I watched my lord Ariston's eyes fix and focus on the dandy Persian commander. Like a crazed leopard he sprang at him, his white horse clearing the distance in moments with the speed of an avalanche. My own mare's legs struggled up the muddy riverbank just in time for me to skewer one of the Persian's own guardians in the back as he turned to bar Ariston's charge.

The Persian commander himself had turned to flee, but Ariston was on him. He slammed his javelin into the man's throat with such force it knocked him clean from his fine stallion, spraying Ariston's white charger with an arching jet of hot blood. My prince jumped down on the stricken Persian from his horse, only to be punched square in the teeth by the dying man. Ariston spat out a tooth as the bleeding Persian wrestled from the dust on top of him. The Persian's blood gushed over Ariston as the two brawled on the hard-baked earth. It was only when the Persian's life strength drained that Ariston was able to draw his kopis and finish the man. Then up and off he galloped excitedly looking for King Alexander, cradling the dead Persian's head in hand.

THE CRESENT-SHAPED PELTA CAME IN A RANGE OF NATURAL MATERIALS AND STRIKING DESIGNS.

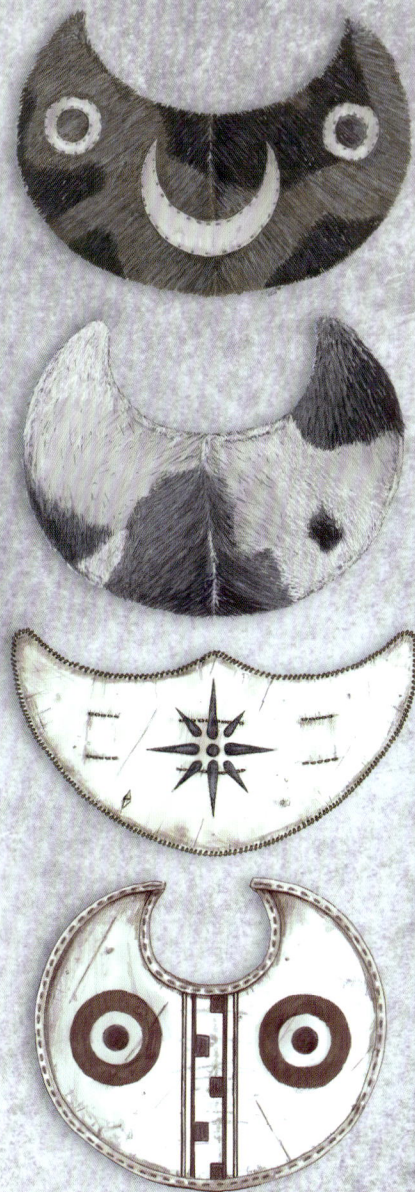

CLOTHING

The Paeonian wears a long-sleeved tunic made of lightweight natural linen. Long sleeves had become the fashion among the Macedonian cavalry units and this rider has followed the trend. Over this linen base garment is an expensive purple tunic, it is a visual signal of him being a royal bodyguard.

BOOTS

The rider wears the famous Thracian boot style with its distinctive flaps. The soft leather boots would help stop the discomfort and chafing of the legs against the coarse hair on the horse's flanks uncovered by the horse's blanket. No stirrups had been invented at this time so the rider's legs would

have to grip the animal's sides to help control the beast. The high boots would help stop nasty rashes forming on the rider's skin. Vase paintings show different lacing systems were used to secure the leather boot to the owner, with the flaps also having slight design differences as fashions changed over time.

This style and variations of it became common place in many Greek cavalry units, adopted by the elite Athenian and Thessalian squadrons.

PELTA SHIELD

His shield is the Thracian-style light pelta made of woven wicker and stretched cowhide. Stitched on its facing is a stylized animal face (commonly

seen in vase paintings depicting the Thracian Peltast), made of painted leather with two polished bronze discs for eyes. This light, crescent-shaped shield would deflect incoming projectiles and impacts, perfect for fast, light troops able to duck and dodge out of harm's way, but useless in a compact shield wall against heavy infantry. Wicker and willow were popular for shield making as it was tough, and lighter and far cheaper than a bronze-covered shield. Thracian, Amazon (Scythian girls) and Persian warriors are seen in vase paintings carrying the distinctive crescent shield. Clearly it was a popular and widespread design from Thrace to Bactria and beyond for a long period of time.

THRACIAN PELTAST OFFICER. THE PERSIAN GATES, WINTER 330 BC.

This warrior is a mid-ranking commander of a unit of Thracians from the Triballian kingdom allied to Alexander the Great. His warband of light infantry peltasts are from a mountainous region of Thrace (modern day Bulgaria); they are ideal troops for alpine combat. The Thracian has been tasked with hunting down Persian troops under the command of Ariobarzanes on the lower slopes of the Iranian Zagros Mountains. Dislodging Ariobarzanes and his stubborn Persian defenders from their mountain strongholds was key to ending the bitter fight for the vital pass through the mountains. Controlling and clearing the mountains of Persian resistance would open the door to the huge riches of the Persian city of Persepolis.

THE PELTAST AND LIGHT CAVALRY

The Thracian peoples were famous for their horsemen and their light infantry or peltasts; both types were lightly armed, favouring mobility over cumbersome, heavy protection.

Carrying two or more javelins and a light pelta shield (from which they get their name), the peltast was a fast and nimble skirmish fighter, as was the similarly armed Thracian light cavalryman. Easily recognizable on the battlefield due to their striking cloaks, the peltasts and the light cavalry would be employed to protect an army's flanks or to scout ahead of the main force when on the march. During the early stages of battle, the peltasts and slingers would dash forward and launch their javelins and lead shot. This would soften up and disrupt the enemy formations before the heavy infantry smashed into the battered enemy line. Then from the flanks the Thracian horsemen would charge in, exploiting any weakness, chasing down enemy cavalry or scattered infantry with lightning speed.

A Thracian warrior could easily expect employment as a mercenary, with the promise of rich plunder and high adventure. Warriors flocked to the camps of well-paying masters, eager to make a name for themselves like the heroes of old. Caring little for their employer's politics, they switched sides when things went bad or if the pay dried up like any good mercenary. The Thracians were regarded as barbaric, coarse and uncouth. Their brute savagery would see them given dark work, the fighting men of Thrace would happily commit cruel, devastating acts, killing everything from livestock to women and children. True barbarians, their murderous traits earned them a fearsome name and a high price tag.

Thracians and their neighbouring peoples, like the Paeonians and Illyrians, lived tribal lives in their native lands. Life among high snow-capped mountains, valleys and plains, harsh winters and roasting summers, bred a rough people.

Tribal rivalry, infighting and skulduggery meant that Thrace was never truly united under one banner, much to the relief of the Greeks and later Romans. The Thracian tribes were said to be so heavily populated that any united army would simply flood over into the surrounding lands and Greek territories, washing away resistance in a wild tide of blood.

THE THRACIAN CLOAK

Horsemen and infantry from the Thracian territories of the earlier classical periods wore a cloak called a zeira. The traditional and colourful Thracian zeira was of a heavy wool or linen. The striking and versatile garment would give a good degree of protection from missile weapons such as arrows, javelin and lead slingshot. Holding one end of the long cloak up with the same hand used to grip the shield makes the thick cloak hang like a heavy curtain, screening the body. It would slow the enemy projectiles, absorbing the kinetic energy before any nasty injury could be inflicted, just like the curtains hung from the hoplite Argive shields.

Its colours and striking patterns may have been a tribal mark similar to Scottish clan tartan, or a personal recognition system, like a coat of arms on a medieval knight's tabard. Being of wool it would, of course, be of great use at keeping a warrior warm during the cold Thracian weather, and act as a blanket at night.

POSSIBLE DESIGNS OF ZEIRA CLOAKS. DYE COLOUR AND COMPLEXITY OF THE WEAVE WOULD INCREASE THE COST OF THE CLOAK. ONLY NATURAL PLANT- AND ANIMAL-BASED DYES WOULD HAVE BEEN AVAILABLE. THIS WOULD LIMIT THE INTENSITY OF THE COLOUR AND WOULD SEE A FADING OUT WITH EXPOSURE TO THE ELEMENTS. ONLY THE RICH ELITE WOULD BE ABLE TO RENEW THEIR COLOURFUL ATTIRE, WHILE THE EVERYDAY FOLK'S CLOTHING WOULD BE FADED AND SUN-BLEACHED FROM A LIFE OF LABOUR OUTDOORS.

HELMET

The warrior wears a Thracian-style helmet made of bronze. Its cheek guards are also in bronze and hang from hinges which are riveted to the helmet's inner rim. They are expertly crafted to look like a moustache with mouth and lips; they follow the shape of the face, curving to protect the nose. The whole face is well protected by these cheek pieces, which make it more of a split face mask. They are commonly seen on surviving examples of Thracian helmets, with some examples showing highly detailed, lifelike beard styles created by master metal workers of the age. This type of helmet would require huge skill and talent on the maker's part to create its complex shape. It would thus be an expensive piece of the warrior's panoply. Mounting points for crest boxes and plume holders can be found on surviving helmets of this type.

Under the tall helmet the warrior wears a rough, shaggy felt Thracian cap as a liner.

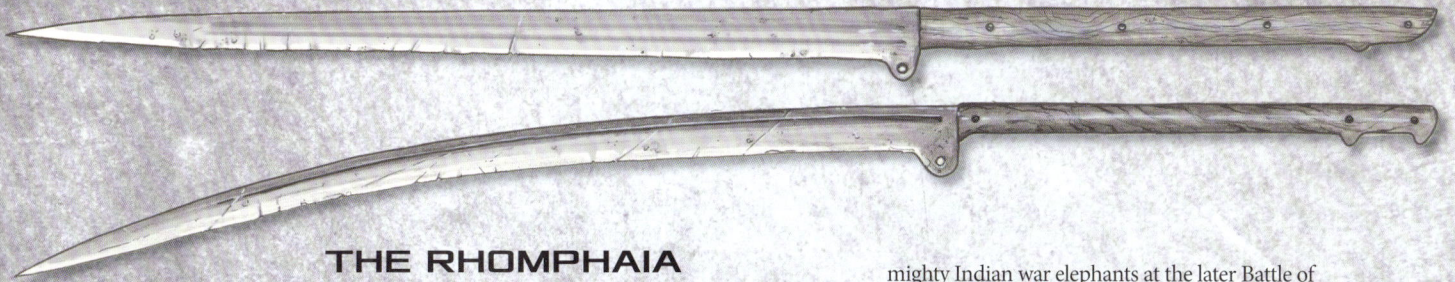

THE RHOMPHAIA

The warrior carries the fearful rhomphaia, a weapon with a long, single-edged iron blade; it was unlike any other blade of the period. Its narrow, slender blade ends at the long, wooden haft grip, which allows space for the two-handed grip needed to put full force into the attack. It looked more like some form of farmer's sickle. The rhomphaia was a hacking weapon and would inflict hellish injuries, capable of lopping arms, legs and heads off with one swing. This weapon would make easy work of enemy cavalry, chopping off horses' legs, sending their riders crashing to the ground to be finished off by one more swing of this nasty blade. Such blades proved of great use against the feared and mighty Indian war elephants at the later Battle of the Hydaspes in 326BC. The disadvantage of using the rhomphaia was that it needed both hands to use it, leaving no free hand to carry a shield to defend against counter-attacks, one deadly and heavy strike had to take down the enemy first.

Later styles of this brutish weapon (known as the falx) were used by the Dacians against the Roman legions. The carnage it created forced the Romans to reinforce their helmets and add fully segmented iron arm guards to their already formidable war gear.

This Thracian carries his curved rhomphaia in a scabbard of leather and is carried via a sling worn over the shoulder.

THE SLING

Our warrior also carries a weapon favoured by nimble skirmish troops, the simple sling. Made of leather and cord, the sling was used to launch projectiles over great distance with multiplied force. Most peasant folk would know how to use this most-basic shepherd's weapon to ward off wolves from their flocks of goats and sheep. Alongside this is a deep leather pouch to carry the heavy stone and lead shot needed. Molten lead was poured into moulds to form sleek, almond-shaped shot; this shape was aerodynamic and thus better at cutting through the air. By swinging the loaded sling around at speed and letting go of one of the cords at the right moment, the shot was released and zipped forth at the enemy. The heavy lead projectile would slam into the target with terrible force, like a modern bullet. It was capable of smashing bones, rupturing organs and causing internal bleeding on impact, in some cases penetrating the flesh. Effective up to 400 metres this simple, cheap weapon was as deadly as any bow. And wearing metal helmets and body armour was no guarantee of protection from a direct strike by a lead bullet or a stone; a heavy, blunt percussive hit to a helmeted head could still kill a man.

SHIELD

The warrior carries a type of shield called a thureos. This model was a more substantial shield, semi-oval in shape and made from wood. It was far heavier than the traditional wicker pelta. The shield's timber body is covered with stretched rawhide leather to add extra strength. The rawhide is stretched and nailed in place while wet and, once dry, becomes an extremely hard top layer. This style became more popular among the Thracians during the Hellenistic age, and was adopted by later Greek and Roman cavalry units. Its long curved central spine is of wood and is covered at the shield's centre by way of a polished iron boss. This boss is riveted in place, making it the shield's strong point. Painted shields of this type are known to have existed but lacked the traditional stylized animal designs of the smaller pelta shield. The warrior carries the shield by holding a handgrip which is carved into the back of the shield's centre boss.

CLOTHING

The warrior wears a fine cloak of wool in the Thessalian style. Its tips are weighted with bronze beads to help keep it in place; in this he has chosen to emulate his Greek paymaster's style, perhaps to gain favour around camp and shake off the uncouth reputation of his fellow Thracians. His traditional zeira cloak has been relegated to his bed mat and is carried rolled up and hung from his belt. His base garment is a long-sleeved tunic made of thick red wool. This expensive garment was payed for with the plunder collected while in the employment of Alexander the Great. The red garment is covered with a well-worn black tunic. The two garments are belted at the waist with a plain sash of purple wool, robbed from one of his Persian victims. The simple leather belt holds a small leather pouch.

On his feet are the high Thracian-style boots. Made of leather, these boots, once insulated with dry grass or perhaps fleece, offer a degree of protection from the winter weather. Some method of waterproofing the leather, such as natural wax or oils, may also have been used.

THRACIAN PELTAST

My boys were raggy lads, not a pot to piss in between the lot of 'em. Then their kid king, one-eyed Phil's brat, says 'come with us, i'll make ya all filthy rich!' He did not lie! Look at us now, all fancy 'n' fat on meats, strutting about full of coin and wine like little kings.

I heard one of them Bessi lads got himself a proper fine purple 'n' yellow tunic off some posh Persian he slotted. Not a rip or drop of guts on it. Then this Bessi lad's brother stabbed him in the eye for it! Bloody animals that Bessi lot.

THE BATTLE OF THE PERSIAN GATES, WINTER 330 BC.

This man is an officer of the Persian King Darius' Achaemenid Empire and is a member of the elite Persian Immortals. He watches over the deadly ambush on Alexander the Great's army, an army that has blundered into the well-planned and prepared trap devised by the Persian king's commander, Ariobarzanes.

Ariobarzanes was satrap of the city of Persepolis and was responsible for the defense of the city, which held the gold reserve of the whole of the Empire. A successful holding action at the pass would give King Darius the time he needed to build a new army from his remaining loyal territories. This fresh army was desperately needed after his defeat at Gaugamela.

The trap was set in the narrow mountain pass which runs through the Iranian Zagros Mountains. This pass was a one-way-in, one-way-out trail, surrounded by high cliffs and sheer rock walls.

Deeper and deeper the Macedonians marched into the gloom of the ever-narrowing snow-filled pass. If Alexander had sent out scouts, they clearly never made it back to warn their countrymen of the trap.

When Alexander's men entered the narrowest point of the pass, Ariobarzanes' trap was sprung. The Persian warriors, hungry for payback after so many defeats, rained a storm of arrows and rocks down upon their boxed-in foe. Unable to find cover or retreat due to the bottleneck in the claustrophobic pass, Alexander took heavy losses. The Greek and Macedonians were easy prey for the smaller Persian force that dominated the high ground. Entire units of men where simply crushed under boulders and buried under rockslides triggered by the Persians perching high above them.

Fallen men struggled to claw a way out, dragging their smashed, torn limbs, only to be trampled into the frozen rock by the mass of fleeing men.

So murderous and hellish was this opening to the battle that Alexander had to do the unthinkable, abandon the wounded and leave the dead men for the crows, an act of great disrespect in Greek culture.

It took around a month to destroy the avenging Persian force on the high, frozen peaks. Alexander suffered very heavy losses at the Battle of the Persian gates, but ultimately won the highest of prizes, the wonderful city of Persepolis and its vast gold-filled treasury.

Ariobarzanes' men at the Persian Gates may have been a guard unit of the Immortals from Persepolis itself. The satrap would have taken picked veterans and local guerilla fighters up into the snowy Zagros Mountain range to ready the pass for their ambush and prepare for a long, bitter fight.

PERSIAN ROYAL STANDARD

The warrior carries a royal Persian standard. On it sits a gold Persian falcon on a field of red-painted wood. From this wooden plaque hang four leather strips, each holding a set of golden disc appliqués decorated with Achaemenid floral designs. It is fitted to a stout spear shaft, which has a butt-spike at its end. This standard is a symbol of Persian power and military pride. It would be a rallying point for the Persian troops and used for unit identification when the massive Persian armies formed up ready for battle. Greek pottery paintings point to these standards as being of a solid construction, not like the large, wind-catching cloth flags of later ages.

Motifs included a four-pointed star design and a bold square design made up of four triangles, two being dark in colour, and two being light. No exact colour scheme for this type of standard is known, but without a doubt they would have been required to be eye-catching.

This standard could well be the commander Ariobarzanes' own personal standard, carried by this most-trusted, loyal officer.

TWO VARIANTS OF PERSIAN MILITARY STANDARDS HELD HIGH ABOVE THE FIGHTING FOR ALL TO SEE. THE PERSIAN TROOPS WOULD USE THE STRIKING STANDARDS AS RALLY POINTS DURING BATTLE.

THE PERSIAN HOOD

The warrior wears upon his head the Persian hood, made of felt and cloth. It's similar to the Phrygian cap in style with its tall point folded down flat. A flap at the back falls to cover the neck. At the front, on the left and right sides of the face, hang the cheek flaps which wrap and tie under the chin. A headband is worn to help hold the hood in place. Under this hood is worn a wrapped scarf covering the mouth and lower face, just as Bedouin Arabs still wrap their heads today to stop dust and grit from soiling their beards and hair. It would appear going into battle without a helmet on was quite normal for the Persian combatants. In the year 401 BC the Persian Prince Cyrus the Younger, while fighting for the throne against his older brother King Artaxerxes II, rode into combat with no helmet, according to the Greek mercenary Xenophon. Then, while in close combat with his brother, Cyrus was killed by a solid javelin strike to the eye.

THE KANTUS COAT

The Immortal wears a long robe-like garment known as a kantus, which could also be hung as a cloak off the shoulder (as seen in the Abdalonymus Sarcophagus). It was made of expensive, thick purple and yellow wool. The sleeves were cut long and narrow as was the fashion. Similar surviving Scythian coats, found in frozen graves, show excellent workmanship and exquisite detail. On its inside, the coat is lined with rich, silky animal pelts. The kantus is trimmed with fine leopard skin, making it a flamboyant, eyecatching garment. The thick insulating wool and fur made it the perfect clothing for cold weather. A piece of clothing like this robe would be worn by the wealthy upper ranks of Persian society and gifted by the king to his favourites and visiting envoys.

GLOVES

The Immortal wears a pair of sheepskin mittens to keep his hands from suffering the bitter cold winds in the high mountain passes. Such hand protection is known to have been available to the ancients as good examples have been found in the frozen Scythian tombs of the Siberian steppe.

THE SPARABARA

The Persian army was known to use a system of archer and spearman combo or sparabara as it was called; the spearmen defended the archer from attack, while the archers launched a hail of arrows. The dathapatis (spearman) would carry a large rectangle shield called a spara. The spara was made of leather and willow shoots and was lightweight; bold, striking patterns could be achieved by the weaving of the willow or osier (which was painted or stained) into the ready-cut leather. This large, tough shield was propped up with a stand to create a kind of mobile fence or screen, from behind which the dathabam (archer) and spearman could fight.

The spear used by the dathapatis was 6 feet long, similar to the Greek dory, but had a distinct ball-shape counter weight at its end. Elite units such as the Immortals had golden apple- and pomegranate-shaped counterweights, while lesser units may well have used bronze or iron.

Unlike Greek armies who used their hoplite or phalangite infantry as their main fighting force, the Persians would field massed ranks of archers, filling the sky with clouds of arrows, raining death from a distance. This is a sound tactic when lacking your own highly trained and armoured troops like the Greek heavy infantry. The Persian archer began training at a young age; primarily this training would be for sport and hunting. The non-elite archer units where recruited or conscripted by their local satraps (governors) and tribal leaders to serve the Persian king when needed. Mostly undisciplined in military matters, and more accustomed to farming and trading, they all had years of practice with the bow. This common skill made a farmer and his bow just as useful to their king as a professional warrior.

Protected behind the wall of spara shields and spearmen,

THE SPARA SHIELD. WHEN USED EN MASSE THE TALL SHIELDS BECAME A MOBILE BARRICADE SCREENING THE TROOPS BEHIND IT FROM ATTACK.

these conscripted men would simply be required to keep on shooting volley after volley of arrows towards the advancing enemy (the need for accuracy was replaced with the need for volume). This saturation of the foe with a constant downpour of arrows would break most formations from a distance. At this point in the battle the Persian cavalry would sweep in and finish the broken enemy units.

The bow was the powerful recurve composite type. Time consuming and expensive to make, these bows would have been greatly prized. It is unclear if all Persian archers where equipped with this high-tech bow, but it is unlikely that the poorer peasant conscripts would have had such costly equipment, instead cheaper, heavier bows must have been used to launch their arrows.

With a good archer using it, the composite bow was accurate up to 50 metres, but still deadly up to and past 100 metres in a massed, indirect hail of arrows. The expensive bow was carried in a bow case similar to the Scythian gorytos to protect it from the eastern elements.

THE IMMORTALS

The name Immortal is misleading as the 10,000 fighting men that made up the legendary force were indeed mortal men of flesh and blood, handpicked for their fighting skills and noble blood lines, not indestructible supersoldiers. Their regiments were immortal only in the sense that when a warrior was killed in action or succumbed to illness or retirement, his place in the ranks was immediately filled by a new picked man. Thus, the elite unit was kept at a full and constant fighting strength.

Each Immortal regiment or 'hazarabam' was 1,000 men strong; 10 hazarabam regiments made up what was known as the 'haivarabam', the famed 10,000. This force was made up of archers, spearmen and cavalry. Some of the spearmen were known as apple-bearers due to the golden, ball-shaped counterweight at the end of their 6ft spears, others had silver, gold and bronze pomegranate spear butts.

The Persian Immortal carries on his left side an iron xiphos sword of Greek design and manufacture. The sword's long, double-edged blade made it a good weapon for mounted combat. Its length allowed the warrior a greater striking reach while seated on a horse, or while riding high up on a camel. Down the blade's centre runs a raised ridge, which adds strength to the metal's length. Its handgrip is made of two wooden pieces. These parts clamped together (with rivets) around the sword's iron tang (which is a bar of iron that extends from the blade). At the end of the tang sits a wooden pommel, which is held snug by an iron finial.

The sword's wooden scabbard has been given a skin of red-dyed leather to add strength and protection to its structure. Strips of bronze could also be fitted along the scabbard's tapered edge to act as extra reinforcement. The length of the wooden case has had a set of fine golden studs fitted. The mouth at the top and the chape at the scabbard's end are made from carved wood and have been painted a crisp white to complement the red leather. Both sword and scabbard fittings could be made from carved ivory, bone and cast bronze. The scabbard hangs across the warrior's body via a shoulder strap (or baldric) made of leather, and sits on the right side of the body so as not to clash with the large bow case worn on the left. This leather is then looped and stitched through a pair of bronze rings. The leather has been stained with a rich purple dye and has only just started to fade under the sun's glare.

Weapons trade between the Western Greek world and the Persian Empire of the East would have made blade types such as the kopis and xiphos available to Persian customers.

Persian warriors also used the dagger-like short sword known as the akinaka. This weapon was similar in style to Scythian blades, and was carried in its wooden scabbard, hung from a belt and lashed to the right thigh. Surviving examples of akinakes and their scabbards are beautifully decorated with gold and would have been real

POLISHED BRONZE-FACED PELTA SHIELD WITH COMPLEX DESIGNS TOOLED INTO THE THIN METAL SKIN.

symbols of the warrior elite's wealth.

Battleaxes are also known to have been employed by the Persian military, just as they were among the Scythian.

He carries at his side, in its carry case, his bow and a complement of iron- and bronze-tipped arrows. The Persians also used the powerful composite bow along with heavier, less-sophisticated bows. The bow case is made of leather and is relatively simple in design. It consists of two parts, the main housing (in which the bow and arrows sit separated via a large leather pocket), and the cover end. This cover could be moved off and away to extract the bow and its arrows. The cover end, at the end of its graceful curved tip, has a stylized bird's head fitted; it is made of thin iron. An example of a fitting of this style made in bronze can be seen at the Ashmolean museum in Oxford. They are a common feature on Persian bow cases seen in the stone relief work at Persepolis in Iran. The bow case is carried slung over the shoulder and hangs low at waist level for easy-to-reach access and could also be hung from the belt.

BARBARIAN DRESS OF THE EASTERN WORLD

The Eastern cultures of the fifth and fourth centuries BC had developed intricate textiles and garments, out-styling Greek peoples of the West.

While the Greeks wore their simple rectangles of linen and wool cloth belted and pinned in place, the Eastern peoples (both Persian and Scythian cultures) had created

garments of far-more-sophisticated construction.

Long-sleeved tunics, shirts, trousers and coats were being worn. These garments could be made using a wide range of fabrics, furs and leathers.

Cottons from India, silks from the Far East, fine wools and the exquisite silky pelts of rare and predatory animals where all incorporated. Vase paintings depict the bold and striking geometric designs worn by the Eastern peoples of Scythia and the Persian Empire, but these pictorial depictions lack any hints as to the colour range used in their clothing.

It is in the frozen tombs and graves of the Scythian cultures that clues can be found as to the colour pallets used. Natural dyes and pigments could transform a plain wool yarn into a host of colours. Once the wool was dyed and dried it could be woven together using complex techniques to create incredible patterns and images in the cloth.

Textile fragments from the Scythian burial mounds of Siberia have survived, frozen in time. Locked in the permafrost, these remnants of cloth show a range of colour could be produced. Dyes from insects, plants and animals where achieved. Greens, blues, yellows, reds, oranges and purples are all present in the surviving fabrics.

Animal pelts are also found to have been popular and common in garment construction. Their preparation and application show the finest craftsmanship. Sourcing these animals for use in clothing would have been no easy task. Dozens of skins may have been needed for one item of dress alone. Certain animals would be rarer, and their value high. Other animals would be desired for their winter coats, so the time of year would dictate the pelts available to the makers. Then there are the real dangers of hunting the predators like Iranian cheetah, leopard and wolf; the risk involved would make these skins very costly. Royalty and the nobility would clad their garments with the more-expensive pelts like beaver, leopard, sable and Siberian weasel. The lesser common folk would wear the skins of the animals they tended, like goat, camel, horse and sheep, and whatever they could catch.

The use of dye was also employed in the preparation of animal pelts by the Scythians. An example of such dying can be seen on a Scythian man's squirrel fur coat at the State Hermitage Museum in St Petersburg, Russia. The squirrel fur was dyed purple, and would have made the pelt look very exotic, perhaps even supernatural. This would have given the owner a unique and eye-catching style. Such style would be of great importance to a king or chieftain wanting to impress or intimidate his rivals.

This same squirrel coat shows that the use of gold leaf was also included in its construction. It also has intricate patterns and figures finely cut into leather, which was then painstakingly sewn onto the remarkable garment using the smallest of stitches.

The wearing of just the chest half of the bronze cuirass was said to stop the wearer from turning his back to the enemy. This was a practice Alexander the Great used to shame his own Macedonian officers who failed to hold their ground.

To this Persian warrior, wearing the breastplate only is more practical as it is less weight for his legs to carry up and down the high mountains; he has no intention of running from this battle.

The half cuirass or 'hemithorakion' is a muscled torso design, a style that remained in fashion from the Classical Period to the late Roman Empire.

The two types of armour worn, plus the element of surprise and owning the high ground, would make this warrior hard to dislodge from his prepared ambush site.

BODY ARMOUR

The cold winter weather of the Iranian mountains has made the Persian wisely double up on his armour. The base layer armour is a quilted, padded linen vest with a skirt of padded pteryges. Its outer layer of cloth is dyed a rich expensive yellow,

The multiple layers of linen which make up the vest help to give the garment similar protective qualities to stiffer composite armour types, offering a good degree of protection from the effects of blunt trauma like the later medieval arming jacket and gambeson. The vest has more flexibility and can be worn closer to the body; this would help keep the wearer warm in the winter months.

Weather conditions have a big impact on how a soldier wears his equipment. It is said that the Persians wore their armour under their rich, colourful robes, which may have been a simple way to counter the effects of the heating of the metal armour by the hot Middle Eastern summer sun. Winter may have seen a reverse in the layering of clothing and armour to limit the effects of bone-chilling temperatures on the wearer.

On top of the quilted vest he wears a Greek style bronze half muscle cuirass. This metal armour is held in place by a set of leather straps and buckles fed through bronze rings.

THE UNIFORM

The warrior wears a pair of long, thick, red-wool trousers tucked into his wool socks. Trousers were commonplace among the Persian and Eastern peoples and were regarded as the dress of the barbarian by the Greeks. A long-sleeved tunic dyed in the expensive royal colour purple covers his torso. Traces of coloured paints have been found on the Abdalonymus Sarcophagus, which depicts a number of Persian troops in a wealth of coloured garments. This man wears a cross-section of the colours from the Abdalonymus stonework.

The purple tunic has a central panel of white down its middle, known to be a mark of royal dress. This indicates his senior rank and status among the men conducting Ariobarzanes' deadly ambush.

With Persia holding so much wealth, the kings would issue their troops with uniforms made of expensive dyed fabrics. The effect of the eye-catching colours on an enemy's mindset could be highly intimidating. To see a Persian army appear from the dust clad in costly purples, yellows and reds was a clear visual message from the king to an enemy that he commanded vast wealth and huge power. The Persian treasury at Persepolis, was not only filled with gold and silver, it was also a great storehouse of woven treasures, fabrics dyed in super-expensive sea purples, saffron yellow and rich reds equal in value to any gemstone. To wear it projected power and strength.

FOOTWEAR

On his feet the warrior has chosen low-cut, solid leather boots to wear, far more suitable for mountain trekking than the fine blue court shoes seen in the Abdalonymus Sarcophagus. They have studded soles, allowing a better grip on the snow-dusted mountain trails which Ariobarzanus had them fighting in.

The feet of humans 2,000 years ago would have been far tougher than the feet we have today in the Western world; we spend a lifetime in comfortable, protective footwear, leaving adults with the same soft, fleshy feet as young children, unprepared and unaccustomed to their natural job of walking on hard, bare earth. For a Persian or a Greek warrior to clad their already tough feet in leather boots or sandals would have added more to his ability to travel quickly over harsh, broken ground for weeks on end without too many foot problems – vital when marching an army to battle.

PERSIAN IMMORTAL

Their song echoed merrily up from the deep gloom. The wind had dropped, and a flurry of snow fell gently down into the pass. Then in the distance a harsh trumpet call rang out from below; in moments the singing stopped, replaced by the gruff barking of commands, then for a moment silence fell. To my left a heavy rumbling sound grew into the mighty resonating thunder of a large rockslide. This was my lord Ariobarzanes slamming the Persian gates down on the invaders. The calamitous din slowly faded into the distant twisted screams of men.

I nodded to my snow-dusted archers, crouching in their rocky perches, and stood up. Stepping forward to the edge I looked down the sheer rock face into the frozen mist. My eyes caught sight of movement. It was the polished glinting of hundreds of metal shields and helmets; they looked like a river of bronze filling the floor of the pass. At seeing the mass of trapped enemy, I nudged a large rock over the cliff edge with my boot. It tumbled and spun on its way down, knocking and churning up other rubble and razor-edged shards as it bounced its way down onto the Greek men. This was my signal! All around me my men sent their arrows streaking down, piles of rocks were set loose, crashing down the rocky walls into the deep, narrow pass. The sound was hideous and glorious, it was a good start to the day.

INSIDE ITS PROTECTIVE LEATHER CARRY CASE SITS A COMPOSITE BOW AND A CLUTCH OF BRONZE-TIPPED ARROWS. THE CASE COULD BE HUNG FROM A BELT OR CARRIED OVER THE SHOULDER ON A SLING.

THE BACTRIAN REVOLT 329 BC.

A heavily armoured rider such as this warrior would ride among the elite shock cavalry of a tribal war host. Highly disciplined professional bodyguards to their kings and tribal leaders, these men would be of high-ranking social status among their kinfolk.

Like other horse cultures, the Scythian people wandered vast areas of land in a pastoral life. From the Black Sea to beyond the Altai Mountains of Siberia, the Scythian cultures blossomed.

Tribal grievances and conflict meant a life of combat. Scalp-taking was an old practice among the nomadic Scythians. Stories of cloaks made of stitched human scalps and drinking cups crafted from enemy skulls added to their fearsome reputation.

It was among the Scythians that the legend of the Amazons has its origin, as the young Scythian girls fought alongside their men. To a Greek warrior, being killed at the hands of a young girl was a shameful end.

The Scythians loved to adorn themselves with fine gold metalwork in the unique animalistic art form known as the 'zoomorphic style'. Stunning golden treasures (equal to those of the Egyptian pharaohs) found in their ancient burial mounds have shown that they employed master metalworkers from the trading cities and outposts along the Black Sea coast to create these magnificent, iconic works of art. They also adorned their skins with zoomorphic tattoos. Mummified remains from their frozen Siberian graves show wonderful beasts and monsters wrapped around their bodies.

According to the Roman historian Curtius, in the year 329 BC, while campaigning in the lands of Bactria and Sogdiana, (a vast region that spans today's Afghanistan, Uzbekistan and Tajikistan), the Macedonian king Alexander the Great was forced to send a column of Greek cavalry and a large force of infantry to restore order and control to the region around a city called Maracanda. The province's tribes had revolted against Alexander's forces occupying their lands and were on the warpath. They had destroyed the Macedonian garrison stationed in the city and had become a real danger to Alexander's rule.

The Greek relief column was wiped out in a bloody ambush by Scythian, Sogdian and Bactrian warriors led by the rebel Persian commander Spitamenes as they marched towards the citadel of Maracanda.

Of the 800 Greek mercenary riders sent out on that mission by Alexander, only a handful made it back across the barren wilderness to friendly territory.

The catastrophe spooked the so-far-undefeated Alexander to the point of threatening the survivors with death if they spread word of the massacre. A year earlier, Alexander's general Zopyrion and his army had met the same fate at the hands of Scythian tribes at Olbia by the Black Sea. News of this second murderous bloodbath by the Scythian peoples would sap the moral of Alexander's Macedonians and add to the fearsome legend of the warlike nomads.

Spitamenes, with his horse-archer Scythians, Bactrians and other allied warriors returned to their base at the newly captured city of Maracanda, filled with fresh confidence from their victory over the Macedonians. Alexander could not allow Spitamenes

any opportunity to create more bloody resistance and personally led an army out to destroy him. For four days they marched and covered the distance to Maracanda only to find the entire rebel Scythian and Bactrian force had dispersed from the citadel, along with Alexander's new nemesis, Spitamenes, into the vastness of Bactria.

All Alexander could do was punish the local traitors who had harboured and aided Spitamenes. He executed all their men and set the region on fire.

A TROPHY OF BLOOD

In his fist the warrior clenches a fresh, gruesome war trophy, the scalp of a defeated enemy. Such a trophy would be hung from his war gear as a macabre decoration and a visual warning of his murderous capabilities.

LEFT, ZOOMORPHIC IMAGERY COVERS THE WOODEN CORE OF THIS IRON-STRIP-FACED PELTA-TYPE SHIELD

SCYTHIAN HELMET

This Scythian warrior wears a converted bronze Illyrian helmet. It has had bronze scale cheek guards added to its Illyrian bowl. The drawing was inspired by the modified Greek helmet from a burial find at Nymphaeum (which was one of four Greek trading colonies) in the ancient Crimea. This region alone has six known Scythian burial tumuli in close proximity to the Greek outposts: a clear indication of the cultural blend, wealth and military power which thrived in this part of the Scythian world.

A belt of overlapping iron plates carries the distinctive tools of the Scythian: the bow case, known as a 'gorytos', and the sword in its eared leather scabbard. Some Scythian kings clad their scabbards with beautifully detailed golden facing plates. The multiple metal plates have been sewn with strong sinew to a leather backing and edged with goatskin. At the front opening, two bronze, Greek-style, bull's-head decorations have been applied.

LAMELLAR LEG ARMOUR

Hung from the inside of the body armour is a pair of hard leather lamellar armoured chaps. Hard yet flexible, the layered leather-plated chaps would offer excellent protection to a mounted rider's legs, which are the easiest part of the body for a dismounted warrior to attack. Bronze and iron scale leg armour of this type, along with Greek style greaves, were also worn by the Scythian nomads.

WEAPONS OF WAR

This warrior carries a javelin, sword and the powerful recurved Scythian bow in its gorytus. This gorytus was a combined bow case and quiver used by the Scythian to transport and protect the bow. Tribal leaders and kings would clad their bow cases with beautiful golden plates depicting heroic battle scenes and stories. The gorytos could hold in its quiver compartment up to twenty-five iron-, bronze- and bone-tipped arrows. Some of the Scythian cultures are believed to have used poison-tipped arrows for combat, turning normally survivable wounds from their arrows into a lingering, feverish death. They painted the fletched end of the arrow shaft with colourful designs mimicking the patterns of the snake from which the venom was taken, leaving the arrows for hunting and sport painted in other quickly recognizable patterns.

The Scythian bow was a composite type made from laminated wood and animal horn. Its complex construction created a powerful, compact weapon, perfect for mounted archery. The bow was the primary weapon of the warrior; he could fire around twelve arrows per minute while riding at speed on his horse.

The double-edged iron sword is carried in its unique eared scabbard made of tooled leather and embellished with a zoomorphic panther appliqué.

He could also carry a javelin which can be used as a missile weapon or a short lance if needed.

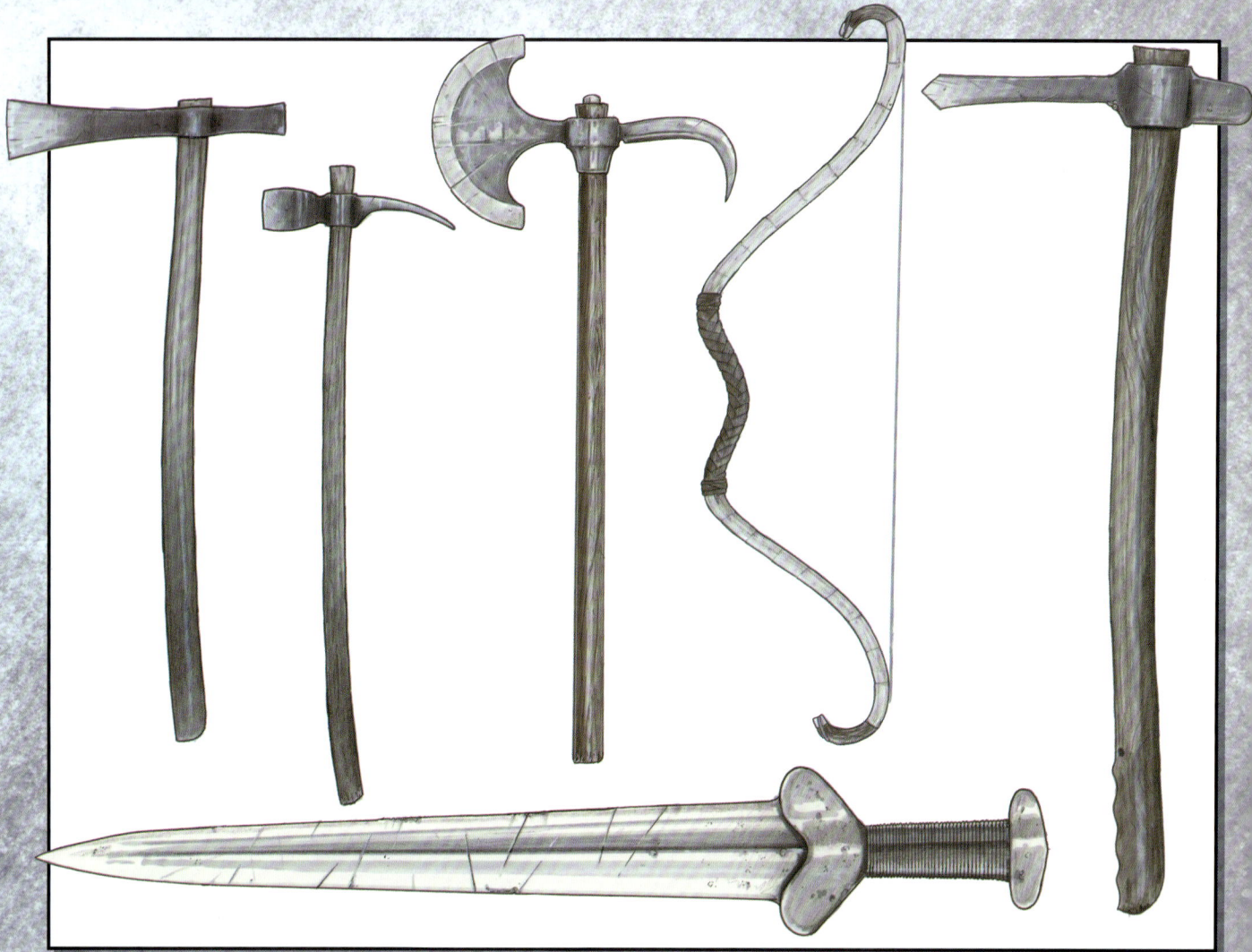

A SELECTION OF WEAPONS FAVOURED BY THE MOUNTED SCYTHIAN WARRIORS: THE BATTLEAXE AND SAGARIS AXE, THE POWERFUL AND COMPACT COMPOSITE BOW AND SWORD. SUCH WEAPON TYPES WERE ALSO EMPLOYED BY THE FIGHTING MEN OF THE PERSIAN EMPIRE.

SCYTHIAN ARROWHEADS CAST IN BRONZE. NOTE THE BARBED TYPE; THIS WOULD BE A DIFFICULT OBJECT TO REMOVE FROM THE CASUALTY'S BODY WITHOUT MORE TISSUE DAMAGE, BLOOD LOSS AND PAIN. ONCE THE ARROW HEAD WAS REMOVED, THE WARRIOR WOULD THEN HAVE TO SURVIVE THE INFECTIONS THAT CAN ACCOMPANY SUCH DEEP TISSUE WOUNDS.

The clothing worn by the Scythians was practical as life on the steppe meant hot, burning summer weather and freezing winters. A tunic of fine wool, long, plain-linen trousers and simple, soft-leather ankle boots are worn by this man. Highly patterned and colourful woven fabrics were very popular among the nomads too; the high quality of the fine workmanship of such garments was held in high regard by their Persian neighbours. On his tunic (which is trimmed with hare fur) the warrior sports multiple eagle appliqués made from thin moulded gold, which have been stitched down the length of each sleeve.

On his head he wears a leather Phrygian cap, padded with felt. This hat was commonly worn by the Scythian and other Eastern peoples alike. Scythian burial finds show that metal scales and plates could also be fitted to this type of hat to armour the head. This superstitious warrior wears a predatory cat motif on his cap for luck.

This rider wears a linen-based armour (the linothorax), its yoke and chest have been reinforced by the addition of bronze and iron scale armour. The use of metal scale armour was very popular among the Scythians due to its flexibility and no doubt its attractive look. In bright sunshine the dazzling light would reflect off the polished metal scales, blinding the enemy and giving the swift horsemen a gleaming magical aura.

Under the right side of the body armour is a plate of bronze, laminated to the linen under a panel of leather. This right side of the armour was unprotected by the shield, so it was common to see scale and plate armour added to the underarm area.

Bands of tooled, geometric patterned leather adorn the armour's chest and waistband. Alongside this decorated leather the warrior has fitted a golden deer, a truly quintessential Scythian zoomorphic motif. Such animalistic decoration was believed to be a form of magical charm used to keep bad spirits at bay.

The linothorax has a heavy leather skirt of pteryges to protect the abdomen while allowing free movement at the hip and waist.

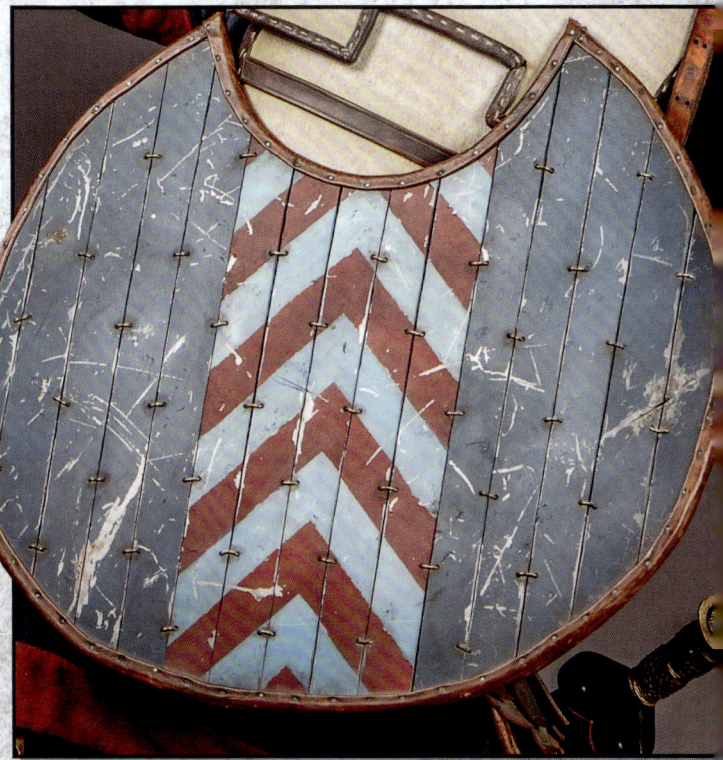

SCYTHIAN AMAZON

WESTERN SCYTHIAN PRINCES, ANCIENT CRIMEA.

You Greek men of the West, you entomb yourselves behind your stone-walled cities talking of freedom. Freedom? What do you know of freedom? Your lives are slaved to possession of land and walls. I am a hawk high above, free on the wind, slaved to nothing.

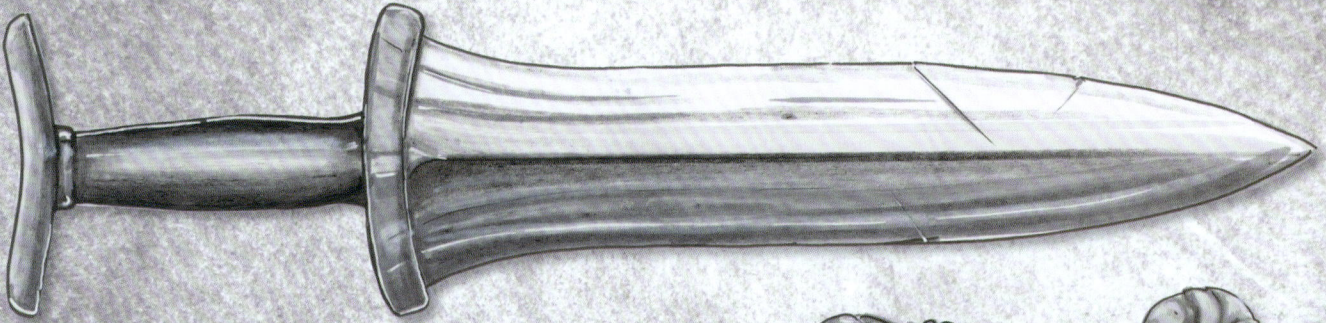

According to the writings of the Greek historian Herodotus, the Scythian word for Amazon was 'Oiorpata', meaning 'man-killer'.

Fanciful tales of tribes of warrior women cutting off their breasts to make it easier to shoot with the bow can be dismissed as total nonsense. To remove large amounts of flesh would be painfully dangerous to the individual and would weaken the muscle. Death rates from such acts would be far too high to make it sustainable. Modern female archers have never needed such surgery to win gold at the Olympics.

More likely is that these seemingly breastless Amazon women where pre-pubescent Scythian girls, fighting alongside their male kin. In a world where horseback fighting was commonplace, once the girls and boys could ride they would need to defend themselves and their herds of livestock (on which they depended for food) from predatory animals, bandits and raiding enemies. It is totally possible that a young Scythian girl, trained in the use of a bow, would be as important as the boys were to the defensive strength of her people. After all, a killing shot from a young girl's bow is still a killing shot.

Once puberty hit, marriage and motherhood would no doubt follow. The young female riders would retire from their guard-like duties to raise the next generation, returning to defend their interests alongside the men when need arose. These were mothers living hard lives in harsh unforgiving environments, equal to their men in combat. To the ancient Greek this equality was an alien concept and the Amazon legend fascinated them. Many hundreds of vase paintings depict the Amazon girls dressed and equipped the same as their men with typical Scythian and Persian panoply.

BRONZE DAGGERS IN THE ZOOMORPHIC STYLE: SOPHISTICATED METAL WORKING TECHNIQUES WOULD HAVE BEEN EMPLOYED IN THEIR CONSTRUCTION.

IRON-PLATED BELT

Like the male Scythian warrior, the Amazon wears at her waist an iron-plated belt, which would carry her fighting equipment. Her dagger is made of cast bronze and is carried in a tooled-leather sheath. The sheath is strapped around the thigh to stop it shifting while riding at speed. The dagger's handle has a zoomorphic design of two bird heads at its top and two boar-like beasts at its base. Two boar-tusk pendants are also carried. Such decorations would also be added to her horse's leather bridles.

A fine fur pouch hangs alongside her gear; this carries a ration of cheese. With all the milk-producing livestock available to the nomad Scythians, horse, goat and cow cheese would have been on the menu. Preserved cheese has been found in frozen Scythian tombs (but its taste is unknown). The fur pouch has a small zoomorphic horse plaque fitted.

SAGARIS BATTLEAXE

A long, wooden-handled sagaris battleaxe is carried from a secondary belt sitting under the iron-plate belt. The leather axe holder has golden appliqués fitted. The axe was a common weapon among the nomad Scythians. Its long shaft gave a better reach and the bronze axehead's weight would multiply the force in a swinging attack. The axe's cutting blade has a sharp pick-like point at its other end. Such weapons would inflict terrible wounds, and instant kills if impacting an enemy skull. Grave finds show strikes to the head from such weapons were a relatively common cause of death for the Scythian warriors. Horses found buried with their dead masters show that they were dispatched to follow them to the afterlife with blows to the skull from such pointed axes.

THE GORYTOS BOW CASE

The Amazon carries her compact composite bow stowed in its leather quiver/bow case (the gorytos, as it is known). This type is made to completely cover the precious bow and its arrows, weatherproofing it from the harsh conditions of the steppe. Shielding it from the mud and dust kicked up by her horse would help to keep the expensive bow serviceable. This practically designed gorytos has an eye-catching panel of painted and patterned leather framing a mythical golden griffin plaque.

SHIELD

The shield is a very light wood and leather type perfect for cavalry. This style of woven shield was common among the nomad cultures. Painted wooden sticks have been woven into the hide to form an attractive pattern. The weaving of the wood into the leather creates a strong, flexible, and robust arrow-stopping shield. The Amazon carries her shield slung to protect her back. A leather hand grip and arm loop are fitted to allow the shield to be held while holding the horse's reins. The young Amazon has hung a fox tail from the shield for decoration (perhaps a memorable kill trophy).

Much larger shields made in this way were used by the Persians and called the spara.

NOTE THE EXCELLENT LEVEL OF LAYERED PROTECTION. THE SOLID BRONZE DOME OF HER HELMET, AND THE FLEXIBILITY OF THE BRONZE AND IRON OVERLAPPING-SCALE ARMOUR. THEN THE THICK PADDING OF THE MULTIPLE LAYERS OF LINEN AND LEATHER IN HER BODICE, AND THE LIGHTWEIGHT AND DURABLE WOOD AND LEATHER OF HER SHIELD. EVEN HER BOW CASE PROVIDES AN EXTRA LAYER OF PROTECTION, SHIELDING THE LEFT THIGH OF THE YOUNG WARRIOR WOMAN FROM MISSILE ATTACK. ADD THE SWIFT SPEED OF HER WELL TRAINED HORSE, AND THE HAIL OF ARROWS SHE IS LOBBING AT YOU, AND YOU WOULD FIND HER A VERY HARD TARGET TO HIT.

HELMET

This young Scythian princess wears a converted bronze Chalcidean helmet. It has an overlapping bronze-scale aventail to protect the neck. Her eared Scythian felt cap offers a snug fit and extra padding to her head. The helmet's original bronze cheek guards have been replaced with flexible iron scale cheek guards. The bowl of the helmet has been painted with a striking zoomorphic stag design. On the brow sits a silver zoomorphic goat monster ornament.

BODY ARMOUR

Her body is clad in a thick leather-and-linen padded bodice with side openings. Its chest is reinforced with a field of iron scale plates in a triangular pattern. A golden stag sits centrally on the scale panel. The shoulder guards are also overlapping iron scales to allow the flexibility needed while using the bow and riding at the same time.

LEFT: MULTIPLE LAYERS OF FLEXIBLE PROTECTION COVER THE NECK AND BACK. OVERLAPPING BRONZE AND IRON SCALE ARMOUR, PLUS THE VERY LIGHT ARROW-SNAGGING, WOOD-AND-LEATHER SHIELD WOULD MAKE IT VERY HARD FOR AN ARROW SHOT TO STRIKE FLESH.

THE AMAZONS DRESSED STRIKINGLY FOR COMBAT, CARRYING THE SAME DEADLY PANOPLY OF WAR USED BY THE FIGHTING MEN OF THE SCYTHIAN PEOPLES. THE PRESENCE OF SKILLED FEMALE COMBATANTS ON THE BATTLEFIELD CREATED FEAR AND FASCINATION.

BIBLIOGRAPHY

Agre, Daniel, *The Tumulus of Golyamata Mogila near the Village of Malomirovo and Zlatinitsa* (Avalon Publishing, 2011).

Aldrete, Gregory S., Scott Bartell and Alicia Aldrete, *Reconstructing Ancient Linen Body Armour* (The John Hopkins University Press, 2013).

Alekseev, Andrei, *The Golden Deer of Eurasia* (Yale University Press, 2000).

Cassin-Scott, Jack, *The Greek and Persian Wars 500-323 BC* (Osprey, 1977).

Cernenko, E.V., *The Scythians 700-300 BC* (Osprey, 1983).

Connolly, Peter, *Greece and Rome at War* (Greenhill Books, 1998).

Cunliffe, Barry, *The Scythians: Nomad Warriors of the Steppe* (Oxford University Press, 2019).

Dahm, Murray and Peter Dennis, *Macedonian Phalangite versus Persian Warrior 334-331 BC* (Osprey, 2019).

Dahm, Murray, and Adam Hook, *Athenian Hoplite versus Spartan Hoplite* (Osprey, 2021).

Dahm, Murray, and Seán Ó'Brógáin, *Leuctra 371 BC: The Destruction of Spartan Dominance* (Osprey, 2021).

Fields, Nic, *Thermopylae 480 BC* (Osprey, 2007).

Fields, Nic, *Syracuse 415-413 BC* (Osprey, 2008).

Herodotus, *The Histories*, translated by Tom Holland (Penguin Classics, 2014).

Hovell Minns, Ellis, *The Scythians and Greeks* (Cambridge University Press, 2010).

Jones, Ryan, and Waldemar Heckel et al, *Macedonian Warrior: Alexander's Elite Infantrymen* (Osprey, 2006).

Karasulas, Antony, *Mounted Archers of the Steppe 600 BC–AD1300* (Osprey, 2004).

Loades, Mike, *The Composite Bow* (Osprey, 2016).

Matthew, Christopher, *An Invincible Beast* (Pen & Sword Military, 2015).

McNab, Chris, *Greek Hoplite versus Persian Warrior 499-479 BC* (Osprey, 2018).

Quintus Curtius Rufus, *The History of Alexander*, translated by John Yardley (Penguin Classics, 2004).

Roberts, Rebecca (ed.), *Gold of the Great Steppe: People, Power and Production* (Paul Holberton Publishing, 2021).

Sekunda, Nicholas, and Angus McBride, *The Army of Alexander the Great* (Osprey, 1984).

Sekunda, Nicholas, and Simon Chew, *The Persian Army 560-330 BC* (Osprey, 1992).

Sekunda, Nicholas, and Richard Hook, *The Spartan Army* (Osprey, 1998).

Sekunda, Nicholas, and Angus McBride, *Warriors of Ancient Greece* (Osprey, 1999).

Sekunda, Nicholas, and Adam Hook, *Greek Hoplite 480-323 BC* (Osprey, 2000).

Sekunda, Nicholas, and Richard Hook, *Marathon 490 BC: The First Persian Invasion of Greece* (Osprey, 2002).

Shepherd, William, *Plataea 479 BC* (Osprey, 2012).

Snodgrass, A. M., *Arms and Armour of the Greeks* (Cornell University Press, 1967).

Vickers, Michael, *Scythian and Thracian Antiquities in Oxford* (Ashmolean Handbooks, 2003).

Vuksic, V., and Z. Grbasic, *Cavalry: The History of a Fighting Elite 650 BC-AD 1914* (Arms and Armour Press, 1993).

Webber, Christopher, *The Thracians 700 BC-46 AD* (Osprey, 2001).

Xenophon, *A History of My Times*, translated by George Cawkwell (Penguin Classics, 1979).

Xenophon and H. G. Dakynes, *Anabasis* (Independently Published, 2022).